Killed In Action

Eyewitness Accounts of the Last Moments of 100 Union Soldiers Who Died at Gettysburg.

Gregory A. Coco

"Centuries may pass and new generations populate our land, yet the name of Gettysburg will not fail to call before memory the heroic deeds enacted there."

Captain John E. Reilly
69th Pennsylvania Infantry
September 11, 1889

Copyright © 1992 Gregory A. Coco

Printed and bound in the United States of America

Published by THOMAS PUBLICATIONS, P.O. Box 3031, Gettysburg, Pa. 17325

Library of Congress Catalog Card Number: 91-65484

ISBN-0-939631-47-4

Foreword

On the idle hill of summer,
Sleepy with the flow of streams,
Far I hear the distant drummer
Drumming like a voice in dreams.
Far and near and low and louder
On the roads of earth go by,
Dear to friends and food for powder,
Soldiers marching, all to die.
                                    A.E. Houseman

The impact that Civil War soldiers made on their country has been deepened by their power with the pen. Few soldiers in American history have written accounts of their lives in wartime to match their vividness and insight.

Attracted first by the element of honesty in the stories of the common soldiers who fell at Gettysburg, author Gregory Coco believed a look at their final moments of life would be of interest to a generation to whom the Battle of Gettysburg still holds a fascinating interest.

He began collecting these accounts some years ago when compiling a series of battlefield incidents to be included in his books entitled, *On The Bloodstained Field*.

The soldiers' lives were strange ones, lived in the narrow dimension of the present. They didn't see the future, for it was not there; and if they could not move into it or beyond it, they could not return to their past. They did not have the true languor of young men whose dreams were of worlds ahead of them, and who saw the present only as a prelude to it.

But if they were without a past or a future, and were caught in the present, what they saw there was especially clear. Their accounts may have lacked polish, but their literary power was most striking. Along with descriptive clarity they have dramatic intensity and a sense of honesty of words spoken in the presence of death.

The importance of these accounts lies, moreover, in the abundant light they shed on the ultimate cost of any war: men's lives.

                                    Robert B. Moore
                                    Kansas City, Missouri

Acknowledgments

Writing *Killed in Action* was simply pure pleasure for me. I have always enjoyed research having to do with the life of the average soldier in the Civil War, especially any subject which does not glorify war. The labor of putting the raw materials together, and now to hold the finished piece, pleases me more than I can say. But it was not the effort of a single person. I received generous help and encouragement from many, and must thank from the bottom of my heart, all who assisted me in this project. They are:

Cindy L. Small, for her many long hours of dedicated hard work and skill on the word processor. She also lent editing artistry to the manuscript, before, during and after the creation and completion of her own first book—*The Jennie Wade Story,* a book I highly recommend.

Robert B. Moore, for valuable time sequestered from his busy schedule with the Kansas City Chiefs, to complete a powerful yet beautiful "Foreword," which honored all soldiers, both Union and Confederate, who died at Gettysburg.

William A. Frassanito, for his usual kindness in providing documentation from his private collection on Private Thomas H. Hunt.

David M. Nevins, George W. Letts, and Dr. Joseph M. Dobie for their courtesy in allowing me to use family correspondence and photographs.

Michael Rhode, archivist at the Otis Historical Archives at the National Museum of Health and Medicine, for his efforts in procuring a much needed photograph.

David N. Lewis of the Vigo County public library, Terre Haute, Indiana, for a long and arduous search leading to valuable information on Captain John J.P. Blinn, including his burial site.

Licensed Battlefield Guides and colleagues Roy E. Frampton, Wayne E. Motts, Edward F. Guy, Jr. and James M. Clouse for aid at the National Archives, and for materials shared from their own personal research collections.

Kathleen Georg Harrison, Robert H. Prosperi, Karen L. Finley and Paul M. Shevchuk of the Gettysburg National Military Park for prompt and accommodating day-to-day assistance with problems I often encountered.

And finally, to my friend Dean S. Thomas of Thomas Publications, (and his editor-in-chief Mary J. Hinish) for continued support in this, another of my books, which I trust will have at least a "ghost" of a chance of being somewhat successful.

Photo Credits

Front Cover: Sixth Plate ambrotype and bullet-scarred, bloodstained prayer book of Private John Cassiday (or Cassidy) of Philadelphia, who was mortally wounded on July 3, 1863 near Gettysburg while fighting on Cemetery Ridge against George Pickett's Confederate Division. Accompanying these objects, a letter written in September of 1948, states:

> Private John Cassidy, son of John and Catherine, born in County Mayo, Ireland in 1842. Came to America at the age of 17.
> Volunteered to the Union Cause in 1862, and was assigned to Co. H. 69th Regiment, Pennsylvania.
> During the first [days] battle of Getteysburg, [sic] he was hit by a shot which was deflected by a picture of the Blessed Virgin Mary, which he carried in his soldiers manual over his heart, saving him from death. In the third [days] battle of Getteysburg he was wounded fatally, the shot passing through the same manual he still carried, however, on this fatal day the picture of the blessed Virgin was missing.
>
> Mrs. Anna Schuster

A special thanks to my friend, Curator Paul M. Shevchuk, a witty, knowledgeable, and always helpful gentleman, for bringing this poignant relic to my attention, and on several occasions for assistance with photographing items from the collection at the Gettysburg National Military Park.

Back Cover: Colorized version of the well-known Alexander Gardner photograph showing six dead Federal soldiers a mile or two south of Gettysburg on July 5, 1863. The United States waist belt plate pictured here was worn by Private Chancey Kelsey, Company C, 152nd New York Infantry when he was killed by a musket ball during the Civil War. His name and unit were carved into the back of the buckle. Both items are from the author's personal collection.

Title Page: Pennsylvania regimental battleflag. Original sketch by Cathleen T. Glotfelty, Gettysburg, Pennsylvania.

Other Credits: The Color Episode of the 149 Regt. P.V., pp. 12 and 28; Gettysburg NMP, p. 14; *History of the 24th Michigan*, p. 29; *History of the 44th N.Y. Regt.*, p. 43; *History of the Bucktails*, p. 58; David Neville, p. 61; *History of the 5th Regt. N.H.V.*, p. 62; *History of the 141 Regt. P.V.*, p. 66; *The Story of Our Regiment*, p. 67; *History of the Second Regt. N.H.V.*, p. 68; *Under the Maltese Cross*, p. 75; George W. Letts, p. 86; *The Desolated*

South, p. 87; *History of the 2nd Mass. Inf. Regt.*, p. 88; Lane Studio, p. 90; *History of Battery B, 1st R.I.L.A.*, pp. 91 and 109; Dr. Joseph M. Dobie, p. 92; Otis Historical Archives, National Museum of Health & Medicine, p. 97; *History of the 125th N.Y. State Vols.*, p. 99; David N. Lewis, p. 107; Ontario County (NY) Historical Society, Canadaigua, NY, p. 115; all other photos by the author.

Introduction

"In a war like this one, a man's life is of small account."

The words are appropriate enough...those of General Daniel E. Sickles as he lay dazed and bleeding on a surgeon's crude operating table near a place called Gettysburg, so many long years ago. He instinctively knew that ofttimes an individual in battle, as in life, could make a difference. But Sickles was also consciously aware that, in reality, a battlefield is an intrinsic region where one man's mortal being is indeed, nearly worthless. War is like a great monstrous threshing machine; it does not keep score; it does not pick and choose; it does not show preference. It merely crushes and maims and destroys, with no rhyme or reason, until its bloody, sickening work is done. My inherent belief in the truth of what Sickles uttered on that Thursday, July 2, 1863, is then, the primary motivation for this small book.

A soldier, W.J. Patterson, formerly of the 62nd Pennsylvania Infantry, said it best when he noted in a speech given at Gettysburg in 1889:

"Have the dead been mentioned except in numbers? Have the cripples been referred to except in the aggregate? Yet it was the rank and file that stood the shock of battle and that gave blow for blow. It was the columns of soldiers that charged the enemy or stood like a rock against fierce assaults."[1]

Patterson was correct, of course, except he left out the general, field and line officers who died too, bravely beside and among the men they commanded.

In *Killed in Action* you will get an imperceptible impression of what casualties truly signify in a large battle. Here before you then, are one hundred officers and men—a pittance, really; an almost insignificant number of the over 5,000 Federal soldiers who sacrificed their lives during the Campaign and Battle of Gettysburg. Only one hundred! Try to imagine the size of the book you would be holding, if I had been able to discover the eyewitnessed memories of 5,000 deaths. Or 10,000, if we include Confederates.

Unfortunately this would not only have been impractical, but also impossible. For what you will encounter are the gleanings of research through hundreds of memoirs, regimental histories, letters, newspapers, diaries, and official reports. Most of these papers, if they even mentioned a soldier who was a casualty of Gettysburg, simply and matter-of-factly list his name. I have attempted to find something more personal than that. I wanted a witness to death, a view into the suffering and pain; much more than just a passing notice of "killed in action," or "died of wounds." I wished to make these slain more human, even touchable, if not in person, then at least within the context of our minds.

What confounded me though, was the difficulty of locating lengthy biographical remembrances. It would appear logical that out of almost 5,500 Northern deaths, it should be relatively effortless to find many hundreds. Yet I was, in time, only able to secure about 200. Of those 200, only about 90 or so seemed detailed enough for inclusion within this booklet. I realize that there are many additional sources available that I did not peruse, but I take reassurance in the words of Mr. Patterson again, who said: "Hundreds of papers have been written on this famous battle, yet the one-thousandth part has not and never will be told."[2]

My hope is that you who read this will gain some pleasure and sadness from the final moments of a small group of good and true men. Pleasure in the opportunity to know these men more intimately, and sadness in the brutal fact of their early and tragic deaths. And as the brother of deceased soldier, Thomas Hunt, stated: "If this will influence anyone in any way to help to mitigate war, then I'd like to do it."

We buried them darkly at dead of night,
The sod with our bayonets turning;
By the straggling moonbeams misty light,
And the lanterns dimly burning.
Few and short were the prayers we said,
And we spoke not a word of sorrow;
But we steadfastly gazed on the face of the dead,
And we bitterly thought of the morrow.
But half of our heavy task was done,
When the clock tolled the hour for retiring;
And we heard the distant and random gun
That the foe was sullenly firing.[3]

In the soldiers' biographies beginning presently, you should observe that the men are listed in an approximate chronological order as to when their actual deaths or mortal wounds occurred. For instance, if a dying artilleryman is remembered by a nurse on July 8, he will still be entered in the text on the morning of July 1, let's say, which was the actual date he received his mortal wound. Please be aware that while some of the accounts included may seem painfully brief, it is simply a fact that 90 percent or more of Civil War dead received even less or nothing. And finally, note the use of the Latin "*sic,*" the little flag that indicates the word just used is printed exactly as it was given in the original. I have tried not to overuse this signal, so keep in mind that most quoted pieces are verbatim and may contain factual and stylistic errors.

Gregory A. Coco
Bendersville, PA 17306
November 11, 1991

Part I
Tuesday, June 30 and Wednesday, July 1, 1863

"They charged, those Boys in Blue,
'Mid surging smoke and volleying ball,
The bravest were the first to fall—
To fall for me and you.'[4]

Onward they came; columns upon columns crowded on turnpikes and country roads; men silent and grim with overwhelming fatigue, and uniforms and throats thick with the fine summer dust. The never-to-be-forgotten Pennsylvania campaign of 1863 was in full swing. Hardened veterans of Robert E. Lee's Army of Northern Virginia were even now on Northern soil, and soon would feel the threatening presence of George G. Meade's steadfast and persevering Army of the Potomac. For even at this moment it marched mercilessly forward toward a fateful and historic collision with destiny near Gettysburg, and where soon, the very air would reek with death.[5]

A grim first day saw combat for over ten hours, from the break of morn along the mist-shrouded Chambersburg turnpike, to the culmination of the Union retreat that smoke-clouded evening at Cemetery Hill. The astounding casualties on the first of July totalled upwards of 16,000 bleeding, battered men. Many of the dead and wounded combatants of both armies remained unattended for over four days—a time in which they suffered and bloated and corrupted in the stifling atmosphere surrounding them.

Private Robert H. Clark,
Company B, 7th Maine Infantry, 3rd Brigade,
2nd Division, 6th Corps

With all of the killing that took place at or near Gettysburg, this first soldier was, oddly, not a casualty of musketry or cannon fire. He was like many of the others who, during the eight week Gettysburg Campaign were casualties

9

of disease, heat stroke, mistreatment or accidental causes. Clark's story is of one such incident.

While a portion of the Union Army of the Potomac was about to become engaged in heavy fighting north and west of the town, the Sixth Corps of the Army of the Potomac trudged wearily northward attempting to arrive in time to do service with the rest of the Northern forces, which were all pointed toward Gettysburg. The forced marches of this nearly forty-mile trek wreaked havoc on the bodies of some of the infantrymen.

The Parish Records of the Ascension Church at Westminster in Carroll County, Maryland hold this interesting sidelight to the main battle, which was soon fought thirty miles northward.

> *July 1, 1863-R.H. Clarks [sic] Union Grave Yard*
> Note: The R.H. Clarks whose burial is mentioned above was from Presque Isle, Maine and was at the time of his death in the United States Army. He was brought in an ambulance to McAllen's Hotel, corner of Baltimore and South Streets with the 6th Army Corps (Sedgewick's) *[sic]*, June 30, 1863 and died the same night. He was sun struck on the march from V.[a] to Pa. from the effects of which with exhaustion, he seems to have died. He was not buried at the same hour as the four...[others].... He was buried at about 3:00 p.m. The others were buried at about 9:00 a.m. R.H. Clarks was a member of Co. B. 7th Maine Volunteers....

The company records of the 7th Maine list only two men killed or mortally wounded at Gettysburg. Obviously, Clark was not one of these. However, his passing was as much caused by the Battle of Gettysburg as was any other man's who died in combat on July 1, 2, or 3, 1863.

 ### Corporal Wilson D. Race,
Company A, 149th Pennsylvania Infantry,
2nd Brigade, 3rd Division, 1st Corps

Elizabeth S. Myers gave an interesting account of the death of one soldier shot on July 1 who perished either in her house or nearby in one of the field hospitals of the First Army Corps. Myers was a local teacher who lived on West High Street in Gettysburg. On the first day of battle many Union field hospitals were initially set up in the borough. The overflow of wounded from the churches and other public buildings ended up in a few private dwellings. She stated:

> Wilson Race was wounded on the 2nd [1st], through the lungs, but the wound was of such a nature that the physician entertained hopes of his recovery. I wrote for his father and he came a short time after, intending to take him home as soon as he was able to travel. His father was much excited at the thought of meeting his son under such circumstances that he did not give me sufficient time to inform him of his arrival, but rushed to him and the two wept in each other's arms. He never recovered from the shock, but commenced to decline. His father's business would not allow him to remain more

than a few days, and he started for home, leaving directions with me in reference to Wilson. (At the time another son was engaged at Vicksburg.) Wilson was very calm and spoke but little. In a conversation with me the evening before his death, he remarked, "I have always been governed by religious principles." He died on the 24th and the body was embalmed and sent home.

The 149th claimed 336 casualties out of 450 engaged; most were lost along the Chambersburg Pike on the Edward McPherson farm.

Corporal Joseph B. Ruhl, Company D, 150th Pennsylvania Infantry, 2nd Brigade, 3rd Division, 1st Corps

Sergeant Charles A. Frey, of Company D, who was detached and serving at division headquarters, wrote a reminiscence after the war in which he said:

> The loss in my own company was very heavy and a few days after [the battle], while following up the retreating enemy, I met my regiment. They were a sad looking set of men. There were only about one hundred twenty-five left, and my own company, which went into the fight with fifty-two men, was reduced to twelve or fifteen....Eight of my company were left dead upon the field, twenty were wounded and five taken prisoners. A few were absent on "French leave."

Of two brothers, Corporals Samuel and Joseph B. Ruhl, one was killed in the battle, and the other had to march away leaving him upon the field. Word was sent to the family that Joseph was killed. His sister Sarah, on receiving the sad news, said she would go and bring him home. Ordering two horses hitched to a spring wagon, she started on her mournful journey, and by night of the same day on which she received the news of his death she was many miles on her way towards Gettysburg. Reaching the battlefield, she began the search for his body or, rather, his grave, as he had been buried in the meantime. After a long search she found it, had the body unearthed, and placing it in a coffin conveyed it home, where it was laid to rest in the quiet graveyard by the side of the fields through which he roamed in boyhood days.

Sarah was fortunate indeed to have located Joseph's grave on the battlefield of July 1 where he had been killed. That section of ground was held by the Confederates until July 4, and the burial of U.S. troops there was half-hearted and incomplete at best. Many from that part of the field were to remain forever unknown.

Sergeant Alexander M. Stewart, Company D, 149th Pennsylvania Infantry, 2nd Brigade, 3rd Division, 1st Corps

Elizabeth S. Myers, noted above, was interviewed in 1909 by a Philadelphia newspaper reporter. In the article which followed she gave this account of her first meeting with Sergeant Stewart. The meeting occurred on July 4, as she went to assist the wounded inside a church on High Street in Gettysburg, just east of her house.

> I went into the Catholic church. On pews and floor men lay. The groans of the suffering and dying were heartrending. I knelt beside the first man near the door and asked what I could do. "Nothing," he replied, "I am going to die." I went outside the church and cried. I returned and spoke to the man—he was wounded in the lungs and spine, and there was not the slightest hope for him. The man was Sgt. Alexander Stewart of the 149th Pennsylvania Volunteers. I read a chapter of the Bible to him—it was the last chapter his father had read before he left home. Late in the day, by the surgeon's permission, I had him removed to my father's home. That night we were again ordered to the cellar. We closed the windows and shutters. The air was hot and stifling. I fanned my patient. Sitting there one could hear the shots in the distance. Not feeling comfortable, I arose and changed the position of my chair. A moment later a ball came crashing through the wall and struck the floor on the spot where I had been sitting.

Sergeant Alexander M. Stewart,
149th Pennsylvania Infantry.

The reporter added: "The wounded man died on Monday, July 6. During the following summer the dead man's widow and brother visited the home of the Myers. With the girl who had nursed his brother, the visitor fell in love; there ensued one of the charming romances of the war, and five years later Miss Myers became the bride of the Rev. Mr. Stewart."

Sergeant Stewart had been carried off the field by Private Andrew Crooks of his regiment after being wounded on Wednesday, July 1. The wound had caused complete paralysis of his lower limbs. Stewart was buried in the United Presbyterian graveyard in Gettysburg, very near the church in which his father had been baptized sixty-three years earlier. His home was Clinton, in Allegheny County, Pennsylvania, where Stewart's father eventually took him for final interment.

Sergeant Major Asa W. Blanchard, 19th Indiana Infantry, 1st Brigade, 1st Division, 1st Corps

In a memoir written many years after the Civil War, a hospital steward of the 19th Indiana relived the bravery and death of one of its color guards during the hard fighting which occurred on July 1 just in front of the Lutheran Theological Seminary slightly northwest of Gettysburg. This soldier, Henry Marsh, said that his regiment, "held its position for a long time, [but] it was several times driven back through the groves and fields down to the base of Seminary ridge." During one of those retreats, Marsh recollected:

> When the Regiment was ordered to fall back, some one said to Capt. W.W. Macy, "The flag is down." He answered, "Go and get it." The reply, with an oath was, "I won't do it." Captain Macy then ran back, [was] assisted by 2nd Lieutenant Crockett East, of Co. K., in putting the flag in the shuck, when Lieutenant East was shot dead, bearing it to the earth. Captain Macy was carrying the flag from the field, when Sergeant Major Asa Blanchard came up and demanded it. Macy said, thinking that Blanchard would act rashly, "No, there's been enough men shot with it." Blanchard then appealed to the Colonel, who said to Macy, "Let him have it." As soon as Blanchard received it, he tied the shuck around his body, unfurled the flag, and began waving it at the rebels crying out "Rally, boys." At once he was shot in the groin, an artery being cut. W.M. Jackson, who was next to him, said the blood came in a gush. Blanchard said, "Don't stop for me. Tell mother that I never faltered." Capt. Wm. H. Murray took the shuck from Blanchard's body, sheathed the flag again and started to carry it off, knowing that to do so was almost certain death. Just then Burr M. Clifford, of Co. F, came up and took the flag.

Sergeant Major Blanchard's life must have ebbed quickly. He surely bled to death in minutes, and his corpse may have been buried by the Confederates between July 1 and July 4. Or, it could have decomposed quickly in the heat waiting for Union burial squads to find it days after the Southern army left Adams County. Many eyewitnesses stated that a large number of the dead who were left in rebel hands, including their own, were not interred until the Federal army began its cleanup of the battlefield. Blanchard's present grave site is not known to the author, nor are many others in this book.

Private James C. Perrine, Company I, 2nd Wisconsin Infantry, 1st Brigade, 1st Division, 1st Corps

Sophronia E. Bucklin, a volunteer nurse from Philadelphia, came to Gettysburg two weeks after the battle with the U.S. Sanitary Commission to assist the wounded. She stayed until the last hospital was disbanded in late November, 1863. On August 19, while working at Camp Letterman United States General Hospital, she witnessed the inexcusable death of Private Perrine. Nurse Bucklin vividly recounted:

> One of my boys, from a Wisconsin regiment, whom we called Jimmy, became convalescent, and hourly expected a furlough to go home. He had not yet been taken from the medicine list, and one morning, as usual, took the prescription, but was soon compelled to lie down. He was seized with a deadly coldness, and shivered incessantly; his muscles contracted with jerking movements, and great sweat-drops gathered on his cold forehead.
>
> He sent for me, and, as I entered the ward, looked up and said, "It's all up with me now." I replied that we hoped yet to do something for him, but he shook his head doubtingly, and motioned for me to sit by his bed. The surgeon was summoned, but he could do nothing to break the chill of death, which was slowly stealing over him. He reached for my hand, and retained it, till one by one his senses left him. Just before the last convulsive shiver ran through his veins, one of the attendants took it from his grasp, remarking that it was a bad sign for any one to hold the hand of another when death came to the heart.
>
> He was then too far gone to realize anything, and at eleven o'clock he died. The last prescription, by some awful mistake, was deadly poison, and nothing could have saved him. I had often heard him talk of home and friends, but do not know if they ever learned how he died, when he saw the dear prospect of soon meeting them in the near future.

Perrine, a Dodgeville, Wisconsin resident, was buried on August 20 in Section 4, Grave #29 of the camp cemetery; later he was removed to the National Cemetery. Fighting with the Iron Brigade, he had been wounded on July 1 probably somewhere in or near John Herbst's woodlot, just south of McPherson's farm buildings.

Camp Letterman, which will be mentioned again, was a large semipermanent general hospital established on July 15, 1863 to consolidate the various field hospitals, about fifty that had sprung up around Gettysburg during and after the battle. It cared for approximately 5,000 wounded of both sides, and was closed in late November.

Camp Letterman U.S. General Hospital near Gettysburg, where many of the subjects in this book died. It was in operation from July 15, 1863 through November.

Private Louis Gardner, Company B, 19th Indiana Infantry, 1st Brigade, 1st Division, 1st Corps

The case of Louis Gardner is a pitiful, yet classic example of the pain and suffering experienced by thousands of Gettysburg wounded. Many survived, some did not. Here is the medical history of a Wayne County, Indiana soldier who fought death for almost six months. In the end however, he lost, and became no more than a medical curiosity.

Private Gardiner [sic] Lewis, B, 19th Indiana, aged twenty-two, was wounded at the battle of Gettysburg, July 1, 1863, by a round musket ball, which lodged in the internal condyle of the right femur. On November 27, 1863, he was admitted into Jarvis Hospital, Baltimore, the knee being disorganized and discharging a foetid pus. On December 1st, Acting Assistant Surgeon F. Hinkle excised the articular ends of the tibia and femur, sawing off an inch of the condyle of the femur, and three-fourths of an inch of the head of the tibia. An H incision was employed. At the time of the operation the patient was feverish, anxious, without appetite, and sleepless from intense pain. He did well until several days after the operation, when he had a chill. Chills recurred each alternate day, and other symptoms of purulent infection were manifested. On December 23d, the case terminated fatally. The autopsy revealed metastatic foci in the lungs, and six ounces of pus in the left pleural cavity. The incisions were healed, and the ends of the bones were found in apposition, but no union had occurred. The excised portions of the femur and tibia are preserved in the Army Medical Museum.

Gardner would have suffered one of the first gunshot wounds to an infantryman of the "Iron Brigade." He was hit about mid-morning on July 1. His place of entombment is unknown.

Private Levi Stedman, Company I, 6th Wisconsin Infantry, 1st Brigade, 1st Division, 1st Corps

Levi Stedman, the second tallest man in his regiment, was reported to have been killed outright during a charge of the 6th Wisconsin on the "unfinished railroad cut" in the afternoon of the first day of the Battle of Gettysburg. An officer who became the historian of the regiment, Colonel Rufus Dawes, stated this in 1890 in his now famous book, *Service With The Sixth Wisconsin Volunteers.* One hundred years later, in 1990, another book appeared entitled *In the Bloody Railroad Cut at Gettysburg,* which also quoted a soldier of Company I who wrote:

"They reach the railroad cut and Levi Steadman [sic] drops dead...." Both of these sources appear to be in error. Private Stedman still had about eighteen miserable days to live. Here is how he probably died, as told by a correspondent of the Boston *Recorder.*

In one of my visits to the Court House Hospital, in Gettysburg, I noticed lying in the hall, among many others, an individual of a large and powerful frame. There was something in his countenance that fixed my attention at once, and awakened a special sympathy in his behalf. He had the look of a man who had never known fear, nor asked for help, —he could suffer without a groan and die without a complaint.

In answer to my inquiries, I learned that he was from Wisconsin, and of the Sixth Regiment; he had been wounded on the first of July, and the fatal ball had entered the right breast and passed out near the spine.

He did not ask me, as many others, if I thought he might recover; but said, in answer to an inquiry in regard to his religious hopes,—

"Sir, I am anxious to do everything I can for my soul. I have received no religious education. Can you teach me, and tell me what I must do to be saved?"

I knelt on the floor by his side and endeavored to explain to him the first principles of Christian faith. He told me that during the days and nights that he had been lying wounded and alone, he had been thinking most of the time of his sins against God; much of the time he had despaired of forgiveness. And he wished to know if there was any way in which God could forgive them, for he felt that he himself could do nothing.

I found on proper examination that he did not rely on baptism to save him, but merely wished to obey the divine command, and I hoped, as an humble and penitent sinner, he was entitled to the ordinance.

But in order that he might rest, and have time to think on the subject, I left him, and returned again in an hour. He was expecting me, and earnestly requested me not to forget what I had promised.

I brought one of the surgeons with me and a friendly soldier, and, kneeling by the side of the wounded man, I invoked the presence of the great Sufferer and endeavored to lift the anxious one into the bosom of eternal mercy. I then baptized "Levi Steadman" in the name of the blessed Trinity.

When the ceremony was ended, he said, "I thank you, I thank you; now I will rest."

On the following morning, I came to his bed, but he was asleep, and for many hours, being called away, I was not able to see him; but when I again came to him, he was sensible, and, while suffering the greatest pain, was evidently peaceful.

"Do you still trust in Jesus," I said to him.

"Oh, yes," he replied; "I lean on him; I hope in him alone; pray for me that God may forgive me, and not forsake me in death."

I was again absent for more than a day, visiting the field hospitals, and when I returned, I hastened to the Court House; but when I came to the bed of Steadman, he was not there.

"Where," I said to the man, "is Steadman?"

"He died half an hour ago," was the answer.

"And how did he die?" I asked.

"He was sensible and peaceful to the end, and prayed much that God would not judge him for his sins, but would show him mercy, for the sake of Jesus."

May we not hope that the repenting soldier, like the dying thief, was received that day into the paradise of God?

Stedman was found and possibly first removed to the Lutheran Theological Seminary hospital west of Gettysburg, only a few hundred yards southeast of where he received his mortal wound in the left lung. His Federal service records mark his death at this location on July 19. It is possible that the newspaper reporter confused the courthouse with the seminary, as both were large brick buildings. Stedman's home was Brookville, Wisconsin, and today he rests in the National Cemetery on the Gettysburg battlefield.

Private Stephen C. Crofut, Company D, 17th Connecticut Infantry, 2nd Brigade, 1st Division, 11th Corps

J. Henry Blakeman of Company D, 17th Connecticut was wounded by a rifle ball in the left hip on July 1. His regiment supported Battery G, 4th U.S. Artillery, which had taken position on Blocher's Hill (now called Barlow Knoll), a mile or so north of Gettysburg. In a letter to his mother written from Jarvis U.S. General Hospital in Baltimore, Maryland on August 1, 1863, he testified as to Crofut's death.

> I will write what I know concerning Stephens death. As you know we lay for twenty or thirty minutes supporting a battery and while lying there the officers called for volunteers to pull down a fence that was thought might be in our way and was somewhat exposed to the enemy's shells. Selah, Stephen myself and some others went and pulled it down. After lying down again the battery was firing Stephen says "those are ours, give it to them." These were the last I heard him say as just then we moved towards the rebs and my attention was directed to them. He must have been hit at the same moment that I was, for as soon as I got up I saw him lying near me and under his head a large puddle of blood. I did not go to him for one look at his face satisfied me that he was dead and I could hardly move myself. I suppose he was buried by the rebs as they held the feild *[sic]* and our boys that were over the feild afterwards said the dead were all buried.

Private Crofut resided in Stratford, Connecticut before the war. His grave site today is not known.

Corporal William Egolf, Company E, 84th New York Infantry, 2nd Brigade, 1st Division, 1st Corps

Solomon and Catherine Powers lived on the northeast corner of West High and Washington Streets in Gettysburg with four daughters: Cynthia, Ann Jane, Virginia and Lydia. During the battle they cared for fifteen or sixteen wounded Federal soldiers who were hurt on July 1. Two of those men were injured in the heavy fighting near the "railroad cut." John Howard Wert, a local historian, educator, and former soldier who was a teenager at the time of the battle, knew something of these men and wrote:

There were pathetic scenes, too, at the Powers house during its hospital period, for once and again the dark angel of death hovered over it. Two brothers were amongst the defenders of the flag gathered up by these devoted women—Egolf by name, John and William, members of the brave 14th of Brooklyn, affectionately known through the Army of the Potomac as "Beecher's Baby Pups" and "the Red-legged Devils of Brooklyn."

One was nursed back to life and as the color again mantled his wane cheek, he saw his brother pass into the dark valley by the most awful and dreaded death of all the long catalogue of ills incident to army life, gangrene, which had supervened in his wounded limb with all the tears of hideous pain which the pen refuses to chronicle.

William, aged twenty-three, died on July 18. We can only surmise the horrible scene that "the pen refuses to chronicle," as the gangrene accomplished its corruptible work. Before his death, however, Egolf presented a small hymn book to Catharine Sweney who had helped nurse him during those long, hot July days in 1863. It was kept for many years as a cherished memento of the battle.

Corporal John Walls,
Company E, 24th Michigan Infantry,
1st Brigade, 1st Division, 1st Corps

A Detroit area minister, Reverend George Duffield, Jr. visited the Gettysburg battlefield in early July to assist the many Michigan wounded and see to the burial and recovery of the dead. On July 9, 1863 he wrote to his brother, D.B. Duffield concerning the condition of forty-four Michigan wounded in hospitals surrounding the borough. In this letter, Reverend Duffield listed Walls as "No. 4" and wrote:

> John Walls, shot through the groin; in very great pain, and muttering something indistinctly, which we could not make out. Stimulating him with some of brother Sam's pure brandy; it seemed to rally him, and I found he was saying "O yes! O yes!" as if he was all ready. An Indiana man whose name I could not learn, lay dead beside him, and I am afraid Wall [sic] will soon follow him. In his pocket we found a little memorandum book, soaked through and through [with blood]. The only two records of importance were "Chancellorville [sic], my first fight," "July 1st, the battle of Pennsylvania." P.S. Wall is dead.

Private Walls was quite old for a soldier, even during the Civil War when the average age of a soldier in 1863 was twenty-four. At the time of his death he was forty-two. The chances are good that Walls' body made it home to Michigan due to the charitable work of men like Reverend Duffield.

Private Amos P. Sweet,
Company H, 150th Pennsylvania Infantry,
2nd Brigade, 3rd Division, 1st Corps

The Peter Myers house on West High Street in Gettysburg, as has been noted, was a busy place for many weeks during and after the battle. The family cared for about a dozen wounded U.S. soldiers; one of which, Private Sweet, was injured on July 1 in the right leg. After the leg was amputated, he was cared for in the Myers house until his death on July 15. One of Myers' daughters, Elizabeth, expressed her feelings on his death:

> He had been with us several days and had become very fond of my little sisters. Very frequently they sang for him. His favorite was "There is No Name So Sweet on Earth," at that time a popular Sunday School hymn. He suffered from indigestion, and one night in his restlessness, the bandages became loose. It was after midnight; the nurse, tired out, had fallen asleep, and before we could find a surgeon he was so weakened by loss of blood that he died the next morning. A few days later his wife came. She was young and had never been away from home. When she heard of her husband being wounded, she started for Gettysburg, leaving a babe that he had never seen. She did not know of his death until she came to us, and her grief was heartrending.

Elizabeth Myers, who married Henry F. Stewart, the brother of a soldier, eulogized earlier, said in 1870 that Sweet's last words were, "Tell my wife I am going home." Her narrative continued: "That midnight death scene I shall never forget. Myself and Alexander Stewart's father (who had arrived in the meantime) stood by his bed, the old man with tears in his eyes, exclaimed, 'Oh, had it been but God's will that I could have stood by my son's death bed.'"

Private Sweet is now buried in the National Cemetery only a mile or so southeast of where he died.

Private James M. Daniel, Company I, 27th Pennsylvania Infantry, 1st Brigade, 2nd Division, 11th Corps

It was about noon on July 1 when the 27th formed a line of battle below Cemetery Hill and pushed forward northward to support the First Corps who, on their left, were fighting west of Gettysburg. The regiment became engaged almost immediately and after losing about fourteen men killed or mortally wounded, and being greatly outnumbered, it retreated back to Cemetery Hill. The confusion was terrible. Confederates were everywhere, and many Union soldiers became separated from their units, some to remain missing forever. One of these unfortunate cases was that of Private Daniel. His body when located, was presumably impossible to identify. Many advertisements were placed in local newspapers to aid in the search for lost sons, fathers, husbands or brothers. The following notice, typical of the day, was placed in one of the Gettysburg papers on October 1, 1863 indicating the fact that,

> a long personal search on the part of friends had been at length abandoned as hopelessly unsuccessful. Any person giving information of the grave of James M. Daniel, Twenty seventh regiment, Pennsylvania Volunteers, will

confer a great favor on an afflicted family in Philadelphia. Address, Rev. Thomas F. McClure, Oakland Mills, Juniata County, Pa.

Daniel's military service record does not give any other particulars as to the final disposition of his corpse, or a clue to what happened to him, except that he was "killed in action." It can be assumed that he was hurriedly and impersonably buried by the rebels in an unmarked grave, somewhere on the confused and wrecked battleground of July 1.

Private Theodore A. Weaver, Company C, 153rd Pennsylvania Infantry, 1st Brigade, 1st Division, 11th Corps

In all likelihood, at least until late July, Samuel Weaver of Northampton County, Pennsylvania, still felt some hope for his wounded son. His boy, who had laid in a military hospital near the state capitol for nearly a month seemed to be holding his own against a grievous and painful injury. Then, sometime around July 26 or 27 Mr. Weaver received the following two letters, both written on the same day, the day Private Weaver took a severe turn for the worse.

> Cotton Factory Hospital
> Harrisburg Penn.
> July 23, 1863

Dear Sir
  In the famous battle of Gettysburg, among the wounded was your son Theodore; the ball passed through the hip into the abdomen, inflicting a dangerous wound; he was admitted to this hospital where he still is, on July 16th. I feel it my duty to inform you that his condition is very dangerous, though he may yet recover; he behaves nobly now, as he did, I doubt not, in battle but if you desire to be sure of seeing him, it would be better to come to the hospital as soon as convenient.

> Sincerely yours,
> Carleton A. Shurtleff
> Med. Cadet—U.S.A.

> Cotton Factory Hospital, Harrisburg
> July 23, 1863

Dear Sir,
  I think it my duty as Chaplain of the above Hospital to inform you that your son is fast sinking and may not be alive in 48 hours—I am of opinion that under such circumstances you should be here with him in his dying moments at whatever cost or trouble—as you can so well afford to come and help to administer christian comfort.
  I expect you will therefore hasten here at once on receipt of this. Do not delay a moment. In case he dies before you arrive we won't know what disposition to make of the body unless you telegraph to the surgeon (Dr.

Woods, Factory Hospital, Harrisburg) in charge.

I rejoice to find that your son has been religiously brought up and is a professed Christian.

> Yours respectfully
> W.H.D. Hatton
> Chaplain, U.S. Army
> Harrisburg, Pa.

Theodore did not survive that day, and by the time his father travelled to Harrisburg, young Weaver's body was among so many who now were moldering into dust, in the loamy earth of their beloved Pennsylvania.

Captain Stephen C. Whitehouse, Company K, 16th Maine Infantry, 1st Brigade, 2nd Division, 1st Corps

About 11:30 a.m. or 12:00 noon, after a three-hour march, the 16th Maine arrived near Gettysburg and took a position just in front of the main Lutheran Theological Seminary building which was just northwest of the village. The 16th, along with the rest of its brigade, threw up a low breastwork here in the shape of a crescent, primarily composed of fence rails and earth. Fighting was in progress along the ridge to the west, and it appeared to the men waiting there at the seminary that this combat was spreading out and beyond to their right flank. Lieutenant Abner Small of the 16th recounted an incident in that moment.

> I recall that as I looked up at the building behind us and saw some officers in the cupola taking a view, I noticed them pointing northerly. [Gen. Henry] Baxter's brigade soon marched off in that direction, and General [John C.] Robinson went with it. Our brigade was left in reserve.
>
> As we waited by the seminary, Captain Whitehouse came to talk with me.
>
> "Adjutant," he said, "I wish I felt as brave and cool as the colonel appears."
>
> "Why, Captain," I said, "he's as scared as any of us. Cheer up! 'Twill soon be over."
>
> He tried to cheer up, and made sad work of it; his face wore a look of foreboding, and his smile was a stiff mockery. While we were talking we heard the command to fall in; and he looked me full in the face and said:
>
> "Good-bye, Adjutant. This is my last fight."

Some time later the brigade was moved northward across the pike along the low ridge to a small grove of trees where Lt. Small said, there "were low heaps of stones....[that] had been hauled from the field and dumped...by some farmer, years back, and among them now were thick bushes. We clambered over the stone heaps and bushes, wheeled to the right, and went up through the trees to a rail fence. This brought us under fire, and some of our men were hit, and Captain Whitehouse was killed."

The captain, as was recited by two other sources, was killed instantly. No one recalled how he was hit or where the missile struck. Whitehouse was in his early 40s, and was married, living in Newcastle, Maine. The adjutant remembered well the command given minutes before the 16th moved away from the seminary that hot, fearful day, a day when his regiment would lose 232 men out of 275 engaged. Colonel Charles W. Tilden called out, "Fall in!" and then "Forward Sixteenth!" Whitehouse turned, repeated the command to his company, and that was the last time that Small saw the captain alive.

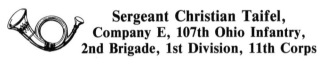

Sergeant Christian Taifel, Company E, 107th Ohio Infantry, 2nd Brigade, 1st Division, 11th Corps

This short biography illustrates some of the complications which often arise when the researcher attempts to track down the final disposition of a Civil War soldier. In the case of Sergeant Taifel, conflicting reports are found as to his death. One, the official source, records that he died on July 18, at Satterlee Military Hospital, Philadelphia, sixteen days after being wounded in the hand on the afternoon of July 1 at Gettysburg. However, the following letter points toward a totally different set of circumstances.

> Navarre, Ohio
> October 3, 1885

Colonel John Bachelder
Gettysburg, Pa.

Dear Sir....

A color bearer of the 107th O.V.I. was shot in the wrist, the ball passing up in his arm [and] stopped near the elbow. He walked around at the 11th Corps Hospital several days and wouldn't let the Doctors cut out the ball. I plead with him one evening when he was frying potatoes and onions to have the ball extricated. He swore he wouldn't and the next morning he was dead. We buried him. When I was at Gettysburg in August I went to the old Spangler Farm where the 11th Corps Hospital was and young Mr. Spangler who lives there told me that the book with the names of those who were buried in the cemetery on their farm had been given to some comrade last summer and that it is now in the war dept or Pension Bureau at Washington....

> A.J. Rider

Alfred J. Rider was regimental postmaster of the 107th Ohio and was twenty-three during the Battle of Gettysburg. He was the soldier who physically buried Brigadier General Lewis Armistead at the George Spangler farm shortly after his death on July 3.

Taifel was twenty-two when he died, and made a fateful decision that day. However, many soldiers' lives were saved by refusing to suffer amputation, and just as many perished by not allowing these serious operations to be performed.

Private Albion B. Mills, Company E, 16th Maine Infantry, 1st Brigade, 2nd Division, 1st Corps

Anna Morris Holstein, a volunteer nurse at Gettysburg, remembered this particular young man for many weeks after the battle. She reported their meeting:

> In the (Union tent), as it was called, standing alone in a rebel row, [of tents] I found a boy of seventeen, wounded and "sick unto death," whose wan, emaciated face, and cheerful endurance of suffering, at once enlisted my sympathy. He was the son of a clergyman in Maine; and in answer to inquiries about his wound, told me, with a feeling of evident pride, that "early in the day his right leg was shattered and left upon Seminary Hill, and he was carried to the rear; that the stump was doing badly; he had enlisted simply because it was his duty to do so; now he had no regret or fear, let the result be as it might." I wrote immediately to his home, to tell them he was sinking rapidly; my next [letter] briefly stated how very near his end was; there were but a few days more of gentle endurance, and the presentiment of the child we had so tenderly cared for proved true— when, with murmured words of "home and heaven," his young life ebbed away— another added to the many thousands given for the life of the nation. One week after his burial his father came; with a heart saddened with his great loss, [he] said that his eldest had fallen at "Malvern Hill," the second was with the army at Fernandina, and Albert *[sic]*, his youngest born, slept with the heroes who had made a worldwide fame at Gettysburg. They were his treasures, but he gave them freely for his country.

Private Mills hailed from Vassalboro, Maine. He was reported to have been wounded in his right leg on July 1. The ball caused an agonizing fracture and the limb had to be amputated at the upper third. He was seventeen or eighteen years old when he died on October 7; the burial followed the next day in the hospital cemetery at Camp Letterman, in Section 9, Grave #3, but the body was shortly moved to the National Cemetery.

Private Daniel H. Purdy, Company C, 17th Connecticut Infantry, 2nd Brigade, 1st Division, 11th Corps

In a report issued in 1864 by the New York State Relief agency of its work done for the wounded after the Battle of Gettysburg, this sad scene was described:

> In looking back upon that battle-field, we know not which most to admire, the bravery of our soldiers in the fight, or their patient and cheerful endurance of suffering as they lay wounded at our feet; even while the tide of life was rapidly ebbing, they would rise on their blankets, their countenances brightening with delight, when told that they were remembered at home, and their bravery appreciated by a grateful people.
>
> But pride of success and love of country were not their only sources of

support—there were also those of a religious character.

A young soldier, James Joiner [Joyner, 157th N.Y.] from Cortland county, drew from his side, a bible stained with his own blood, and whispered to us, that it had never been absent from him in battle.

Not far from his tent lay another soldier, Daniel H. Purdy, of Fairfield county, Conn. At nine o'clock at night he was reported to be dying. By the light of a candle held in a reversed bayonet, some of his fellow-soldiers, and a clergyman and others gathered around his tent where he lay upon a bundle of hay. A prayer was offered up by the clergyman that the way of death might not be dark to him.

When the prayer ceased, young Purdy astonished the group around him by quoting text upon text, [of] the most beautiful of all the promises of the christian religion; while repeating these, his ear caught the sound of a familiar hymn sung in a neighboring tent, and his face became radiant with devotion—death was not dark to him.

Private Purdy, from Danbury, Connecticut, had been wounded in the left shoulder and lungs on July 1, on or near the David Blocher farm north of the town. He died on July 15 at the Eleventh Corps hospital on the George Spangler farm; he lay buried there until removed to the National Cemetery where he now rests.

Private John Flye,
Company K, 13th Massachusetts Infantry,
1st Brigade, 2nd Division, 1st Corps

On July 1 while the retreating Union First and Eleventh Corps poured through the streets of Gettysburg, a soldier of the 13th Massachusetts ducked into the Christ Lutheran Church on Chambersburg Street to avoid capture. When the day had ended and the Confederate army occupied the town, Austin Stearns found himself unable to reach the Federal lines which were now south of Gettysburg. During the remainder of the battle he busied himself by assisting the wounded and exploring the village. On July 2 after visiting a grocery store near the "Diamond," as the center square was then named, he recalled this unusual situation:

> On going back towards the church I saw a rebel ambulance standing before the door with several of our Surgeons standing besides it earnestly talking. On getting near I heard they were talking about some one in the ambulance. On looking in I saw there, dressed in a rebel uniform and very weak from the loss of blood, John Flye, the first man of our company hit. I told the surgeons that I knew that man, that we were of the same company, and they immediately ordered him to be taken in. Flye was left on the field, and the rebs finding him, and seeing his clothes covered and growing stiff with blood, had exchanged his pants for one of their own, and brought him in. The surgeons, seeing him in grey, could not believe he was a union soldier. Flye died in a few days.

Private Flye, a blacksmith, from Westborough, but born in New Portland, was twenty-nine years old. He died on July 26, probably still wearing at least part of a filthy Confederate uniform. He is now interred in the Massachusetts' section of the National Cemetery. One wonders what might have happened to John Flye had his comrade Stearns not happened by in time to identify him as a Union soldier.

Sergeant Samuel Comstock, Company K, 17th Connecticut Infantry, 2nd Brigade, 1st Division, 11th Corps

Private Justus M. Silliman, a close friend of Sergeant Comstock, was wounded and captured north of Gettysburg at David Blocher's farm on July 1. Writing home on July 3 from a field hospital in the public school in the borough, he expressed his feelings concerning Comstock, saying: "I am quite anxious about Sam and would like to know how he fares." A few days later on July 7, Silliman wrote again, explaining:

> I am sitting beside Sam, within our own lines in the 11th Corps hospital situated about two miles east [south] of town. our wounded are very numerous and occupy a barn and farm house and several acres of ground....
>
> It has rained here every day for a week and makes it distressing for many of the wounded who have lain on the wet ground without any shelter. I searched for Sam as soon as I arrived here. it was raining quite hard and I finaly [sic] found him lying out in the storm in a puddle of water. I procured a strecher [sic], and with the assistance of others finaly got him in comparatively comfortable quarters where he still remains. he lay on the field of battle all night and part of the next day, when he was taken to the poor house [Adams County Almshouse] where he remained until the fourth, when he was recaptured and sent to this place. the bullet entered his hip just below the back bone and was cut out at the side of his leg. the bone is some splintered but it is believed not broken. he is rather weak but has a good appetite and is in good spirits. his wound is doing well and pains him scarcely any, and although it will be a long time before he will be able to walk I have but little doubt that he will in the end come out all right....
>
> Sam would like to have you send word to Chester [Comstock] that he is doing well. he will try & write in a few days....Sam has been supplied with a shirt and drawers by the [Christian Commission].

On July 15, Silliman told his mother that, "I could have gone soon after the fight but have staied [sic] here to take care of Sam, and suppose have lost what little chance I had of a furlough. Sam is doing well though is quite weak and tired of lying so long in one position. he is in comfortable quarters and has good attention...."

By August 10, Sam Comstock had been moved to the U.S. General Hospital just east of Gettysburg. Both on August 13 and August 19, Private Silliman stated that Samuel was, "getting on slowly," and also on the 19th, a bed sore had broken. September 3 found Sam enjoying wine sent from home and he, "appears to be improving very slowly....His leg is still suspended in a sling and he is obliged to remain in one position, but he is in good spirits though quite weak and thin...."

By September 9 Silliman could report: "Sam is improving very slowly. I have sometime feared he would not recover but at present appearances are more favorable as he is gaining strength and is in good spirits."

However, at 6 p.m. on September 26, 1863, nurse Silliman had to relay bad news to his mother.

"I have just returned from visiting Sam he is failing rapidly and is liable to drop away at any moment, he seemed disinclined to talk and wished to sleep I have made arrangements so that I can have him embalmed. the cost of embalming will be $15.00, box $5.00, Expressage would cost about $24.00...."

Samuel Comstock died on September 27 at Camp Letterman. Fortunately, Private Justus Silliman was able to get the hoped for furlough to New Canaan, Connecticut. He was assigned to transport home the corpse of his dear friend, Sam, whose funeral was held on October 11 at the Congregational Church in that village.

 ## Lieutenant Colonel George W. Arrowsmith, 157th New York Infantry, 1st Brigade, 3rd Division, 11th Corps

On the July 1 march to Gettysburg, with artillery rumbling in the distance, George Arrowsmith, who had been ill for some time, was told by Surgeon H.C. Hendrick not to go into the fight which was expected momentarily. Arrowsmith, then only twenty-three years of age, replied that he felt physically alright and had even gotten over the fear of going into battle. He then added: "I have come to feel that the bullet is not moulded which is to kill me."

The regiment reached Gettysburg about noon and rapidly deployed north of Pennsylvania College. Subsequently, while fighting to stop the advance of Jubal Early's Confederate division which was pushing into the right flank of the Eleventh Corps, Lieutenant Colonel Arrowsmith was struck by a rifle ball in the forehead.

A letter written on July 27 by Colonel P. Brown, Jr. of the 157th summarized the tragic circumstances: "We had been fighting but a short time, when, upon looking to the right, I discovered that the Lieutenant-Colonel was missing. I moved at once to the right and found him lying upon his back, badly wounded in the head, breathing slowly and heavily and evidently insensible....I could stop but a moment...."

Another officer, Captain Frank Place, who was only ten feet from Arrowsmith when he was hit, said that the colonel never stirred after he fell. Place added: "My First Lieutenant, J.A. Coffin, was wounded and left upon the field. He recovered after a while and found Colonel Arrowsmith's body, and took from his person his Delta Kappa Epsilon badge....I believe that the...badge was sent to his brother."

According to his own account, Coffin was also able to save Arrowsmith's revolver, his shoulder straps, one of which was cut by a bullet, and a little book stained with his blood. Just prior to the time Coffin retrieved these articles, a wounded private of the regiment took a ring from Arrowsmith's finger and the colonel's purse containing about $160.00. This enlisted man was later located in a Newark military hospital where the ring and most of the money was recovered.

Dr. Joseph E. Arrowsmith, hearing of his brother's death, hastened to Gettysburg to locate the body. Through the help of Captain George A. Adams, who was wounded and lying in the Eleventh Corps hospital, the grave, which was "just south of the brickyard," was eventually located. A metallic coffin was procured to remove the remains, as they were badly decomposed. After exhumation, Lieutenant Colonel Arrowsmith's body was returned to Middletown, New Jersey where it was buried on July 26 in Fair View Cemetery.

Color Sergeant Henry G. Brehm, Company C, 149th Pennsylvania Infantry, 2nd Brigade, 3rd Division, 1st Corps

A Myerstown, Pennsylvania native, Henry Brehm acquitted himself with great coolness and daring on July 1, and lost his life in the process. Here is his story.

About 2:30 p.m. on that memorable day, the 149th Pennsylvania was one of many Union regiments fighting for its life near and around the Edward A. McPherson farm along the Chambersburg Pike northwest of Gettysburg. John Friddell later related the saga of that small group of confused but dedicated men, *the color guard:*

> a squad of rebels [had] dashed upon them from a nearby wheat field; [and] that when startled by the rebel yell they barely had time to jump to their feet when the enemy was right by them; that one of them laid hold of the National flag in the hands of Brehm, saying "this is mine;" that Brehm said "No, by God it isn't," seized him by the throat and threw him on the ground, but the Sergeant went down too on top of him. that evidently the rebels had not expected any resistance, and so, in anxiety of each one to get one of the flags, they were unprepared for the hot reception given them and which gave our men the advantage; that in a few seconds, the guard having shot the majority of their assailants, and clubbed others, Brehm was on his feet again with his colors and running at the top of his speed for the regiment....

Captain John H. Bassler, also of Company C, who was then a prisoner of the Confederates, continued the narrative:

> Shortly before three o'clock my Regiment and the 150th while heavily engaged in front, were flanked on the left and subjected to a severe cross-fire, making a speedy withdrawal necessary to escape capture or annihilation.

Color Sergeant Henry G. Brehm,
149th Pennsylvania Infantry.

The blue uniforms quickly disappeared, except those of the dead and severely wounded dotting the field, and the men in gray came swarming around the sides of the barn and were in line along the lane and across the pike.

Suddenly there bounded into view one solitary Union soldier. Great Heavens! It is Brehm, our color bearer. Is it possible that he was left in his isolated position until too late to recall him? Yes, there goes the intrepid Sergeant, bare headed, with giant strides, obliquely across the meadow, the colors on his shoulder. My whole soul goes up in supplication to the God of battles for his safety and escape! For oh imagine the rifles leveled at our hero! Oh, the fearful odds against him! Ah! he has safely reached beyond my view and I am beginning to feel that his escape is not impossible. Vain hope! While my gaze was still fixed upon the spot where Brehm had disappeared there came into view a hatless traitor triumphantly bearing our flag, and as the red-haired, freckly-faced captor came near me with his trophy in passing to the rear, I noticed that the greater part of the staff was missing. I learned afterwards that when the Sergeant had almost effected his escape, a fragment of an exploding shell, flying upward, rent the clothes on his back and inflicted wounds from which he died some weeks afterwards. It knocked him over and broke the flag staff; he regained his feet however and though in a delirium of pain as you may well suppose, made another effort to save his precious charge. But a Confederate soldier who had emerged from the north-east corner of Reynold's [Herbst's] grove swooped upon him and the indomitable Brehm was compelled to yield at last....

The brave and resolute Sergeant Brehm died July 9 in a Philadelphia hospital, never to be forgotten by the survivors of the old "Second Bucktails."

Chaplain William C. Way of Detroit, Michigan, tenderly cared for the wounded and dead of the 24th Michigan Infantry. His solicitude made the last hours of many of these soldiers much easier.

Color Sergeant Lewis Bishop, Company C, 154th New York Infantry, 1st Brigade, 2nd Division, 11th Corps

Three different sources tell of another young colorbearer who had previously made his reputation for bravery at the Battle of Chancellorsville, two months earlier. At Gettysburg this man was shot in the left knee, which shattered the bones therein, and resulted in the amputation of the leg.

The first to see Bishop was a New York state relief agent who was visiting the Eleventh Corps hospital about the middle of July. He wrote: "I saw in one tent three soldiers of the 154th who were shot one after another while holding the colors of their regiment. These were Albert Miracle, Louis Bishop and Rickert *[sic]*, all of Cattaraugus County, and I think the name of John A. Burk should be added."

On Friday, July 24, Reverend F.J.F. Schantz visiting the late battlefield to distribute supplies to the wounded, stopped off for a while at the Eleventh Corps hospital where he, "was for some time with Louis Bishop of Pittsburg *[sic]*. He was the bold soldier who would not give up his flag when one of his legs was shot off. He stuck to his flag until he was wounded in the other leg."

Two days later, Private Emory Sweetland of the 154th, commented in a letter home:

Gettysburg, July 26th
Sunday

My Beloved Wife
  Although I can not get a letter from you I have hopes that my letters will

reach you, so I keep writing to you....About a week ago our steward went away & now I am acting steward & ward master at the same time. I don't know how long that I shall stay here. Louis Bishop our color Sergt is dying to day. he is a noble brave man. he went home before the battle of Chancellorsville & was married to a girl at Olean [NY]...the weather is quite warm & the flies verry *[sic]* thick.

So Bishop died, his courage and intrepidity recorded by an unusually large number of eyewitnesses. He was only twenty-five when he died on July 31. His initial burial was on the Spangler farm, but later, just prior to Lincoln's visit in November, Bishop's body was removed to the new Soldiers' National Cemetery on beautiful Cemetery Hill, where his grave is rarely, if ever, specifically visited today.

Private John Aeigle,
Company K, 107th Ohio Infantry,
2nd Brigade, 1st Division, 11th Corps

Private Justus Silliman, in writing to his mother on July 15, 1863, from the field hospital of the Eleventh Corps, conveyed the presence of this soldier... "there is a german here from Tiffan [Tiffin] Ohio, shot through the lungs, the same bullet passing through his legs. he cannot recover as he breathes partially through his wound. his name is John Aiyla *[sic]* 107th Ohio."

The 107th was a mostly German speaking unit organized in August 1862. On July 1 and 3 they lost forty-five men killed and mortally wounded, entering the battle with only a captain, John Lutz, leading the 480 men of the regiment.

The military service records in Washington, D.C. concluded that John Aeigle was shot in the right side on July 2 near Cemetery Hill and died on July 19. He was supposedly buried on the George Bushman farm which was then the major field hospital of the Twelfth Corps. However this is doubtless an error, as Silliman definitely saw him at the Eleventh Corps hospital on the George Spangler farm. Aeigle was thirty-eight years old and is now entombed in the National Cemetery only a few yards southwest of where he was mortally wounded.

Private James Gillen,
Company F, 11th Pennsylvania Infantry,
2nd Brigade, 2nd Division, 1st Corps

A drummer boy of the 28th Pennsylvania went to visit a relative and several friends in the 11th Pennsylvania on the afternoon of July 1, soon after that unit, along with the entire First Corps, had retreated back to the area around Cemetery Hill, one-half mile south of Gettysburg. He said of this visit:

I finally found Fighting Dick Coulter's 11th regiment hugging up against a wall....I sat against a tree and I heard the exciting story of the 11th's important part in the first day's fight. Next thing I knew, a ball struck the tree over my head....Bullets were flying all about us....My life was saved by a shoestring while I was on the knoll there. As I stooped to tie my shoe, a bullet whizzed by me and struck a man named Gillizin *[sic]* in the fleshy part of the thigh. He went over to a corner; had the wound tied up and went along as if nothing bothered him. He was grit, that fellow.

Gillen, who had enlisted at Salem in Westmoreland County in 1861, died shortly after this incident. According to Musician Simpson, Private Gillen apparently did not take the wound seriously and this act of bravado may have cost him his very life.

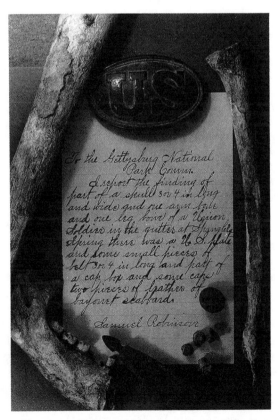

The finding of human remains and lost graves in the Gettysburg area was a common occurrence for many years after the battle. This situation exemplifies the incomplete manner in which burials were conducted, and why so many soldiers killed in action were listed as "unknowns."

Part II
Thursday, July 2, 1863

They laid in every conceivable position among the rocks in that low swampy ground, some crouched behind the rocks as if about to fire, some lying upon their faces, and some stretched upon their backs, like corpses laid out for a funeral, as if they had determined to observe the propriety of attitude even in the hour and article of death. The rains had, during the interval, descended and the hot sun had beat down upon them, and they were now swollen and turned black with mortification, and millions of maggots could be seen rioting upon their flesh. Ah me! thought I, could the fathers, the mothers, and the wives of these unfortunate men suddenly appear and gaze upon the forms they had once fondled in their arms, they would curse to the bitter end the traitors who had brought the desolations and miseries of this war upon their once happy households. [6]

The warm, humid weather of the second day of the Battle of Gettysburg caused many to fall prostrate, overcome with heat and thirst. But so very many more came crashing down, split open and torn, pierced and pelted by the thousands of pounds of iron and lead missiles thrown by Southern and Northern weaponry. Fighting commenced around noon, just west of the old Emmitsburg Road, and continued into the darkness of night, as a poor sickly moon tried valiantly to penetrate the sulphurous air over Culp's and Cemetery Hills. Names and places became famous that day for the foul scenes surrounding them. The Trostle and Weikert and Rose farms; Plum Run and Codori's thicket; peach and apple orchards, streams and woods and wheatfields—all had seared and thundered and crashed; until finally the blood enriched soil was opened to accept the fresh bodies, the torn, innocent flesh of a gored and bleeding Union.

Here are but a few of those 18,000 sacrifices.

Corporal John Ackerman, Company K, 82nd Illinois Infantry, 1st Brigade, 3rd Division, 11th Corps

The state of Illinois had only one infantry regiment present in the Battle of Gettysburg, and that unit suffered but seven men killed and mortally wounded. This death is, therefore, somewhat more lamentable than usual, especially due to the unusual circumstances surrounding it. An officer of the 82nd gave an interesting portrait of the casualty.

Early morning hours on the second day were spent in comparative quiet, each army in full view of the other, and each waiting for the other to begin the fight. The rebels, however, who had possession of the town, had filled the houses standing on the outskirts of the town, just below Cemetery Hill, with sharpshooters for the purpose of picking off our officers, whom they could easily spy standing or walking about on the hill. This had become quite troublesome and General [Carl] Schurz requested Colonel [Edward] Salomon to send a detail of about one hundred men to dislodge the sharpshooters. I had the honor to command that detail, which was made up of volunteers, and stormed those houses, driving out the sharpshooters and keeping possession of the houses the balance of the day. In making up this detail an incident happened which I shall surely remember as long as I live, and I cannot refrain from referring to it at this time. Brave John Ackerman, a private in my company, who on every previous occasion was the first to respond when volunteers were asked for to engage in some daring work, did not come to the front on this occasion. I was surprised at his action, and stepped over to speak to him about it. He said to me:

"Captain, I cannot go with you this time; I feel as though something terrible was going to happen to me today."

He looked pale and despondent. Believing that he did not feel well, I left him, after saying a few encouraging words to him. Within an hour after I left him, Ackerman was killed, a rebel shell cutting off more than half of his head. His remains were buried on Cemetery Hill, close to where he was killed. It is singular, that he is the only one of our regiment killed at Gettysburg, whose name appears on any headstone in the National Cemetery.

The captain was mistaken in one respect. Another 82nd soldier, Ernst Wallischeck, is buried in the Illinois plot of that cemetery.

Ironically, one of the houses "cleared" that morning may have been that of John Louis McClellan and Catharine Freyburger McClain, a brick double house where twenty-four hours later occurred the death of Mary Virginia Wade, the only civilian killed in the Battle of Gettysburg.

Private Albert H. Frost, Company K, 3rd Maine Infantry, 2nd Brigade, 1st Division, 3rd Corps

Private Frost, one of twenty-nine men of the 3rd Maine killed or mortally wounded between July 1 and 3, was a single man from Winthrop, Maine.

His last minutes on earth and burial were observed by a comrade, and still remains one of the most complete descriptions of its kind that I have ever found.

> ALBERT H. FROST was the best and most loved and most patriotic man in the company. In the Battle of Gettysburg the 3rd Maine's position was in the Peach Orchard, in the first line of battle, when we were ordered (214 men and 100 sharpshooters) to go over the Emmitsburg Road [and] down across [a] road to the woods in front of our line of battle, about one half mile. We skirmished into the woods for some distance until the rebels opened fire on us. We found it was Gen. [James] Longstreets Corps that faced us. [actually A.P. Hill's Corps] We stopped and fought them for about 15 min. The last time I saw Albert H. Frost alive I was on one knee and foot loading and firing as fast as I could. Turning around, I saw Frost putting a cap on his rifle. He was behind a small tree about the size of a stove funnel. After that, the rebels tried to get around in our rear to cut our regiment off from getting back to the line of battle. The next thing I heard was the old General's order to fall back double-quick to the Peach Orchard. After the battle was over, I with ANDREW P. BATCHELDER went to the captain and he to the colonel and got permission to go to the woods to find Frost's body and bury it. At that time, there were 48 of our men lying on the battlefield, this being the 2nd day of July 1863. We found him face down and with many others the flesh eaten (in that hot climate) by maggots, but not so bad but that we could recognize him. When we went to bury him, all we could find to dig a grave was an old hoe in a small building. The bottom of the grave was covered with empty knapsacks, then we laid in our beloved brother and covered him with another knapsack, and over all put as much earth as we could find. The grave was dug at the foot of a large tree. We then found a piece of a hard wood box cover and cut his name on it with a jacknife and nailed it to the tree at the head of his grave. He was shot in the groin and bled to death in a short time. The rebels soon stripped him of everything he wore but his shirt and pants. (coat, hat, sox, shoes)

Frost died sometime just after noon on the second of July in an area known as Pitzer's woods. His unit endured casualties of twenty killed, nine mortally wounded, and approximately fifty-two wounded in action. Their colonel was Moses B. Lakeland.

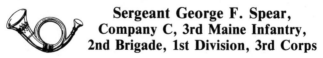 **Sergeant George F. Spear,**
Company C, 3rd Maine Infantry,
2nd Brigade, 1st Division, 3rd Corps

There is somewhat of a mystery attached to this story. In one of my sources Sergeant Spear is reported dead, and in another he is not. Here are the "facts."

Harmon Martin, a Georgia soldier, wrote in a letter to his sister, A.E. Martin on August 25, 1863 from a camp in Virginia:

I am going to send you a trophie *[sic]* that came off of the battle field at Gettysburg. I got three pictures out of a dead Yankee's knapsack and I am going to send you one. If you do not want it you can give it away. The pictures were wraped *[sic]* up in a letter from the person whose image they are. She wrote to the Yankee that they were her picture and she signed her name A. Spears and she lived in Main[e] somewhere but I could not make out where she lived.

Of the approximately 229 Maine volunteers who died as a result of the battle, Sergeant Spear is the only man who meets the criteria established by Martin. He was likely killed or mortally wounded on July 2 around noon when his regiment engaged Wilcox's Alabama brigade just west of Joseph Sherfy's farm in and around Samuel Pitzer's woods along Warfield Ridge. Since the Southern army controlled this section of the field, many of the Maine troops who were hit remained in rebel hands. Spear, possibly one of these men, was reported missing. In his excellent book, *These Honored Dead,* published in 1988, John Busey does not list Sergeant Spear as a casualty. However, in a book printed in 1898 entitled *Maine At Gettysburg,* Spear is, in a revised report of casualties for the 3rd, shown as "killed in action."

Was Confederate soldier Martin correct in his story of the "dead Yankee" from Maine? If the regimental history is correct, but Federal service records as of 1865 do not list him as dead, there of course, may continue to be an enigma here. A possible answer is that he was left on the field, then buried by enemy soldiers after his personal effects were looted. This left no chance for a correctly marked grave site even if the burial squad chose to identify each corpse it found. So then Spear would have been carried on the official rolls as "missing in action" until the regimental update in 1898.

Private Timothy Kearns, Company A, 71st New York Infantry, 2nd Brigade, 2nd Division, 3rd Corps

The chaplain of the 71st almost by accident recalled the death of this thirty-year-old soldier, perhaps one of the first men of that regiment to be hit on July 2. The scene he describes took place between approximately 3:30 and 4:00 p.m. when General James Longstreet's Confederate artillery prepared the way for the attack of McLaws' and Hood's Divisions against the Union left flank.

> The first shell struck not more than two rods behind where I with several other non-combatants were standing, expecting to see [the battle] begin from the front. We all retired rather precipitately to the partial shelter of a brick barn [of Abraham Trostle] hard by and there remained until our artillery silenced the guns that had opened. It was awful. For half an hour it raged incessantly. Grape, canister, solid shot and shell, whizzed and shrieked and tore past us. The trees near by were torn and dismembered. My pack horse was tied to one of them. Twice the poor animal was within a foot of being

The east side and north end of Abraham Trostle's barn, looking westward toward the Emmitsburg Road. Private Timothy Kearns died here at about four in the afternoon on July 2, 1863.

killed, but I did not dare let Mart [his servant] go to bring her behind the barn. A fragment of shell killed two chickens within a rod of where I sat. Every moment I expected to be struck, but at length perceiving that our soldiers had advanced further up the field, the fire was diverted from that point and we were released. I never experienced a deeper sense of deliverance. We retired a little and then the wounded began to come in. One of our boys was brought to us with both legs gone. Poor fellow, he lived but a few minutes, having given me his wife's address and commended his soul to the mercy of heaven. Before he expired a battery from the front again rendered our position unfit for a hospital. The doctors went still further back and as soon as poor Karns [sic] died I followed them.

Kearns, who was from Newark, New Jersey, is buried today in the National Cemetery. In all likelihood his death would have gone unnoted except for this chaplain's misfortune to be caught in that hail of iron so near the front lines.

Sergeant Henry L. Richards, Company F, 2nd United States Sharpshooters, 2nd Brigade, 1st Division, 3rd Corps

During the early afternoon of July 1 the marching column of General Daniel Sickles' Third Army Corps trudged uneasily northward through Maryland. They were aimed straight into Pennsylvania where the Battle of Gettysburg was now well into its sixth hour. It had rained earlier in the day and the roads were now muddy as well as rough. The march was forced, the weather hot, and a few men in the 2nd Sharpshooters were becoming angry, as tempers and nerves frayed. One of those affected, most uncharacteristically, however, is the subject of this sketch. A member of the regiment, Wyman S. White, illustrated this unusual outburst years later:

> [As we marched on]...soldiers kept asking every citizen we met if we had crossed the line and if we were in Pennsylvania.
> Sergeant Richards of our Company, who was generally very careful about finding fault or of grumbling, no matter how uncomfortable things might be, gave the person that said we were in Pennsylvania this answer, "God Damn your Pennsylvania. The rebels ought to destroy the whole state if you can't afford better roads. This road is worse than Virginia roads." Such an outburst from our beloved Sergeant was something very strange indeed. But the forced march over this rough road in the terribly hot sun of that July day was his last march. His losing his temper and speaking out his feelings was a bad omen.

And as if predicted, on July 2 at about four o'clock p.m. the sergeant, who was thirty-seven years old, was shot while fighting to hold back an Alabama brigade somewhere on or near one of the "Round Tops." White continued:

> On the fifth, we received news of Sergeant Richards death. He was [mortally wounded] while we were opposing Longstreet's great charges to capture Little Round Top....He died on the amputating table July 3rd and we were informed that he died from an overdose of either [sic]. He was a noble, patriotic brave man, ever ready to do anything or undergo any hardship for his country. I have before told of his losing his patience and his temper while on the march from Emmitsburg to Gettysburg and his rough remarks to the Pennsylvania woman. That break, being so out of his quiet, courteous ways, seemed to be a forerunner or sign that the worst was to happen to our respected and loved comrade.

Richards' grave is not known to be situated anywhere in the Gettysburg area.

Captain John M. Sell, Company I, 83rd Pennsylvania Infantry, 3rd Brigade, 1st Division, 5th Corps

By all accounts this ill-fated officer should not have been killed at Gettysburg, as his duties placed him in a normally safe position in the rear. And what is also unusual, is that no other officer of that regiment died in the battle, even those on the fighting line. The historian of the regiment tells of this unusual occurrence.

> The only line officer belonging to the Eighty-Third who fell upon this day was Capt. John M. Sell. He was not on duty with the regiment at the time. He had been acting as Provost Marshal of the division since the May previous and on this occasion was engaged in taking charge of prisoners and preventing stragglers from going to the rear. At one time the First and Second Brigade were hard pressed by the enemy, and it became necessary to send

everything to the front that carried a musket. Capt. Sell was ordered to the front with the Provost Guard, and before they had reached there he was struck in the left leg by a solid shot which shattered the limb so badly as to render amputation necessary. From the effects of the amputation he died the next day, and in his death the Eighty-Third lost one of its best officers and most exemplary men.

Captain Sell of Erie had been promoted to his rank in September 1862. Three months afterwards he suffered a first wound at the Battle of Fredericksburg. His burial place may be presently in his hometown, as it does not grace any cemetery in Adams County.

Corporal John Scott,
Company E, 124th New York Infantry,
2nd Brigade, 1st Division, 3rd Corps

The story behind the death of this twenty-one-year-old corporal from Goshen, New York, is made up of the substance from which heroic legends are formed. The 124th New York Infantry made history that second day of July on John Houck's granite-strewn ridge just west of Little Round Top, as it stood among the giant boulders helping to cover the vulnerable left flank of Sickles' Third Corps. In this defense near James Smith's 4th New York Battery, Captain Isaac Nichols and Major James Cromwell had been killed. Former colonel Charles Weygant described the action exactly twenty-one years later, to the day.

> The slope in front was strewn with our dead, and not a few of our severely wounded lay beyond the reach of their unscathed comrades, bleeding, helpless, and some of them dying. One of their number, who lay farthest away, among the rocks near the body of our truly noble and most esteemed Captain Nicoll, could be seen ever and anon, beneath the continually rising smoke of battle, to raise his arm, and feebly wave a blood-covered hand. It was James Scott, of Company B, one of the 10,000 heroes of that great battle. "When Cromwell dashed through the ranks to lead the charge," says one of his comrades, "Scotty was the first to spring forward after him, and when the major fell it seemed to me Scotty changed to a wild beast. He had been wounded in the arm, and his hand and face were covered with blood; but he did not seem to know anything about it, and kept on fighting until a ball hit him in the breast, and went clear through and came out of his back. That must have paralyzed him, for his hands dropped, and, as his gun struck the ground, he fell heavily forward upon it as if he had been killed instantly." But no, Corp. James Scott yet lived. At the time he received the wound in his breast the foe were falling back, and before he recovered consciousness a piece of shell had struck his left arm, near the shoulder (the first wound he received was in the wrist of the same arm), [and] another bullet had passed through his body— entering the left side, breaking two ribs and coming out of the right groin. And yet another piece of shell had struck him in the back, inflicting a most ugly wound and paralyzing every

part of his body, except that right hand and arm which, as consciousness slowly returned, he was waving in token of victory.

Curiously, both the source just quoted, as well as the regimental history of the 124th give the impression that Corporal Scott was only wounded. His military records, however, state that he was indeed "mortally wounded in the chest" on July 2. At this time I do not (but would like to) know the whereabouts of Scott's grave. Sadly, a short while later, the 124th's colonel, A. Van Horne Ellis was also killed in attempting to recover Cromwell's body.

Private Thomas H. Hunt, Company A, 44th New York Infantry, 3rd Brigade, 1st Division, 5th Corps

Hundreds and hundreds of city, small-town and farm people journeyed to Gettysburg for months and even extending into years following the battle. This steady stream of visitors flowed there to locate or to visit the graves of family members who fell during those three fearful July days in 1863. The case of Private Hunt seems to exemplify the situation for many of these heartbroken travellers.

Thomas Hunt was shot in the left leg on July 2, and the wounded member was amputated at the upper third soon thereafter. He died on July 24 or 25 and was buried near a small woods on the Michael Fiscel farm, which had been used as the main hospital of the Fifth Corps for several weeks following the engagement. Hunt, who was a carpenter living in Albany, New York was twenty-seven years old and had enlisted in August of 1862. His family first heard of his wound from a local newspaper. Later, Thomas wrote home cheerfully that he was doing well and would soon be home learning to dance again using his wooden leg. A nurse at the hospital, "Miss Shriver," a fifty-five-year-old schoolteacher, wrote to the Hunt family also, saying that there was no need to come to Gettysburg, as Thomas was well taken care of and they could be of no help. In a letter written from the battlefield on July 4, by Thomas' captain, B.K. Kimberly, he lists the killed and wounded of Company A. In the second-to-last paragraph he said: "Thomas Hunt, leg (since amputated and is doing well)...." Soon after this missive, word came that Thomas was dead. Gangrene had set in; another operation was performed, one after which Thomas sank quickly. His brother, Mark, made his way to Gettysburg in late September of 1863. A description of his melancholy trip follows:

> The president issued a proclamation forbidding bodies' being removed before the first of October. I went down after Thomas's remains, arriving the day before the first of October. It gave me time to look over the battlefield and locate his grave.
>
> The town of Gettysburg was much like a county fair by the first. People were living in tents. Equipment for embalming was to be found. I found a pair of those men going out after a body with the parents of [the] boy

in their rig. I told them of my situation and they asked me to go with them. We arrived at the place where the old people thought their son was buried. The graves were about the size of a city lot. They had been hastily dug, about eighteen inches deep, and bodies laid in side by side with no identification mark. I saw the old parents walk around the awful grave. (This burial was right after the battle.) When we got there some embalmers pointed out the place [where] they thought I'd find my brother's grave. Some graves were marked with a piece of cracker box or stave of a barrel, written in with a lead pencil and almost illegible. I searched that place over without finding the name of my brother.

I saw a pile of clothing on the battlefield, faded by the weather so I couldn't tell whether it was blue or gray. I ran a finger along each side of a button on a suit of clothes to read it and found a body in the clothing. On Seminary Ridge I saw the horse that had been shot under General [George] Meade.

A white farmhouse was pointed out in the distance. They told me there had been a hospital near that farmhouse. It was after dark when I got to the house. The farmer was out doing his chores with his lantern. I asked him if he could help me in my dilemma. He said he hadn't time, but would lend me a lantern and show me where to go. I followed fences as he directed and finally came to an enclosure of rail fence on the edge of the woods. I got over the fence and with the lantern read the little headboards. I found my brother's name cut with a knife. I was satisfied, for I had found what I was seeking.

I went back to the farmhouse and tried to hire the man to take me to town, about seven miles away [about three]. He declined, but told me how to go to get to the [Baltimore] turnpike. I followed the rutted road made by the artillery and then down to the stream. In the stream I saw a light which I surmised was phosphorescence from part of a body. I got across the stream and took the artillery trail again and followed it as directed. Finally I came to a brick house in a grove. When I knocked at the door it was opened two or three inches and I saw there was a chain on it on the inside. I talked with the man a few minutes and found that he wasn't inclined to take me to Gettysburg, but told me how to get to the turnpike, the one the U.S. Army traveled over in going to battle at Gettysburg. So I started out again on foot and finally came to the village of Gettysburg.

I went into a restaurant and got supper. Across the street beside an old ivy-covered church, in the moonlight, I heard some soldier boys singing. I think it was, "Farewell, Mother."

Here is perhaps the proper place to say that one hospital was in operation in Gettysburg at that time. We had sent a box of jellies, etc., to my brother and the day I arrived in Gettysburg I went to the express office and found the box still there. I took it and wanted to distribute it among the sick and wounded in the hospital, but had to go to the Provost Marshal and get a pass for that purpose. I have that pass yet. I took the box in and divided it amongst the men. There was a military guard sustained there all this time. That is how the boys happened to be by the church.

About twelve o'clock I went to a hotel. I was told that during the battle those rooms were used for operations. In several places there were holes where cannon balls had passed through the building. I was taken up into the attic with candlelight and shown my bed. The room was not plastered. I was tired and lay down, but slept very little, because every few minutes there was a scream, or yawk, from something in that room. At dawn I discovered a parrot on a crossbeam.

I think my brother fell in the desperate battle where Pickett made his charge [more likely on Little Round Top]. I saw oak trees shot off by cannons. The country was stripped of fences. The soldiers had used the fences for campfires. Barns were stripped, too. I brought home some relics of the battlefield, but not many; not what I went for. The relics were a bayonet, canteen, and a bombshell. At that time one could take a hayrack and load it full with saddles, blankets, etc., etc....

Next day I went out with a man and knew right where to go. They took the body up out of the grave, and I identified my brother. When the men put [the] remains in the casket, I took [it on] the next train [and left] for home. I had telegraphed on ahead, so the funeral procession assembled at the depot and went right to the cemetary [sic].

If this will influence anyone or in any way help to mitigate war, I'd like to do it.

The official records of the battle state that Thomas Hunt is presently buried in the National Cemetery at Gettysburg in grave G-83 of the New York plot. If Mark Hunt took his brother home for interment, then who now occupies grave G-83? Did Mark Hunt leave the headboard at the Fiscel farm where it was mistakenly placed on another grave? Unfortunately, this mystery is only one of many which surround Civil War burials graveyards everywhere.

Sergeant George W. Buck, Company H, 20th Maine Infantry, 3rd Brigade, 1st Division, 5th Corps

Promoted on his deathbed! This uncommon honor took place during the hot late afternoon of July 2 when Colonel Joshua L. Chamberlain's intrepid regiment helped to hold the Army of the Potomac's left flank at Little Round Top against repeated assaults by portions of E.M. Laws' Brigade, John B. Hood's Division, Army of Northern Virginia. The colonel reminisced that during a pause in the fighting, the 20th moved down the slope of the rocky ridge to care for the wounded and dying so that they might be carried out of harm's way.

In this lull I took a turn over the dismal field to see what could be done for the living, in ranks or recumbent; and came upon a manly form and face I well remembered. He was a sergeant earlier in the field of Antietam and of Fredericksburg; and for refusing to perform some menial personal service for a bullying quartermaster in winter camp, was reduced to the ranks by a commander who had not carefully investigated the case. It was a degradation, and the injustice of it rankled in his high-born spirit. But his well-bred pride would not allow him to ask for justice as a favor. I had kept this in mind, for early action. Now he was lying there, stretched on an open front where a brave stand had been made, face to the sky, a great bullet-hole in the middle of his breast, from which he had loosened the clothing, to ease his breathing, and the rich blood was pouring in a stream. I bent down over him. His face lightened; his lips moved. But I spoke first, "My dear boy, it has gone hard with you. You shall be cared for!" He whispered, "Tell my mother I did not die a coward!" It was the prayer of home-bred manhood poured out with his life-blood. I knew and answered him, "You die a sergeant. I promote you for faithful service and noble courage on the field of Gettysburg!" This was all he wanted. No word more. I had him borne from the field, but his high spirit had passed to its place. It is needless to add that as soon as a piece of parchment could be found after that battle, a warrant was made out promoting George Washington Buck to sergeant in the terms told him; and this evidence placed the sad, proud mother's name on the rolls of the Country's benefactors.

Chamberlain wrote that the dead were gathered "from the sheltered places where they had been borne, and buried...on the southern side of the crest behind their line of battle. Rude headboards, made of ammunition boxes, marked each grave, and bore, rudely but tenderly carved, the name and home of every man." The twenty-year-old Buck from Linneus, Maine was surely among those so carefully interred.

The bodies of the Maine men were eventually removed to the National Cemetery at Gettysburg where today several of them are marked "unknown." The carefully cut headboards in some instances must have been gone unheeded, or were lost or destroyed. The remains of Sergeant Buck, if not removed to his home state by a relative or friend, might well occupy one of these unidentified graves.

 **First Lieutenant Eugene L. Dunham,
Company D, 44th New York Infantry,
3rd Brigade, 1st Division, 5th Corps**

Eugene Dunham was born in Hamilton County, New York on January 18, 1839 and resided in Albany before the war. He was enrolled as First Sergeant of Company D in August, 1861, from which he rose to acting captain of the company several months prior to the Gettysburg Campaign. It was said of him that he possessed a "brave and ardent spirit, with a keen sense of wrong and injustice...."

The specifics of his death and burial are well related in a letter written after the battle by a twenty-eight-year-old sergeant of Company A, Orsel A. Brown.

Camp of 44th Regt. N.Y.V.,
near Emmetsburg *[sic]*, Pa.,
July 6th, 1863.

Mr. A. Dunham,

Dear Sir:

Not knowing as you have learned the painful particulars of the late battle of Gettysburg, it seems a painful duty devolving upon me to inform you of your great loss, and of the deep gloom and sadness hanging over us as a regiment. Lieut E.L Dunham, Company D, 44th Regt. was killed suddenly on Thursday evening, July 2d, at six o'clock while nobly and gallantly urging his men on to duty. He was struck by a minnie [sic] ball under the right eye, and killed instantly. I suppose you to be his father. On leaving camp he gave me your address, and told me I might have to tell you of his death—and dear sir, so it has proved.

Sad is the duty, yet I feel that you will thank me for the few particulars I can write you, and the deep, deep interest I have taken in such a noble man. He fell in our hands, and all his effects are safely in our possession, and when an opportunity is afforded us, will be forwarded to you, if you will give us the directions.

The dear fellow is respectfully buried in his blanket and poncho, and his burial place plainly marked. Captain [Lucius] Larrabee of Company B lies by his side. His (Larrabee's) body fell into the hands of the enemy, and was rifled of everything—many articles of value, $90 in money, &c. He was not found until the next day.

First Lieutenant Eugene L. Dunham,
44th New York Infantry.

As we passed the grave of my best friend on our way to this place I came ahead of the regiment and halted a few minutes to look upon the spot. Freely did the tears course down my cheeks, to think that poor Dunham was never more to be with us; that his well loved form was made to lie low by the hand of some cursed traitor. For your information and my own satisfaction I called at the house near by, and found the general directions as to the vicinity, when in some future time you may recover his remains. He lies in the corner of a fence joining the garden fence; property owned by Leonard Brickest, [Bricker] two and one-half miles from Gettysburg. Enclosed is a leaf of a peach tree under which his body rests.

He was highly appreciated by his company and all officers, particularly the Colonel. Lieut. [Charles] Grannis with myself, tender to you our heartfelt sympathy, at your great bereavement, but be assured that Lieut. Dunham fell in a noble cause, and God has called him home. Sad and lonely without our friends, I cannot but weep with you. I am

Respectfully your obedient servant,
O.C. Brown

 Private James Johnston,
Company K, 4th Michigan Infantry,
2nd Brigade, 1st Division, 5th Corps

This nineteen-year-old man from Shiawasee County, Michigan was among a handful of enlisted men who were fortunate enough to receive very decent burials after the battle. This luxury was normally impossible to hope for as the small details of gravediggers had such an overwhelming task before them.

A close friend of Johnston's, James Houghton, remembered the scene during and after the wild, dreadful fight in and around John Rose's infamous wheatfield. The memoir is left as it was found, with corrections added as needed for clarity.

Our good Old Regiment was now in a criticle Situation there was Rebels Southwest, North, and Northeast of us....Soon the order came to about fase forward double quick march and in less than two minutes our Regiment was passing out acrost the wheat field directly in front of the Rebels, it was here that the crash came a Storm of lead swep through our ranks like hail many of our noble Boys fell to the ground never to rise to their feet again. others were wounded but could hobble a way   our Color Barrer was wounded and droped the flag a Rebel grabed the flag and was in the attempt of carrying it a way when our Colonel [H.H. Jeffords] drew his revolver Shot the Rebel and regained the flag. a moment later a Rebel thrust a bayonet into the Body of our Noble Colonel giving Him a fatal wound about 2 rods south of where this occured my tent mate James Johnston was shot He was but a fiew feet in front of me when He fell. I herd Him Say I am Killed this was the last words that I herd Him speak the rest was groans there was no help for Him.

On July 4, Houghton,

wishing to know that my tent mate was deasently burried I precured a pass for myself and for a fellow by the name of George Tracey...and then started on for the wheat field   when we arived at the wheatfield we found men there busily ingaged in burrying the dead They informed me that they had just got my tent mate burried they showed me His grave His Knapsack and haversack still lying on the ground where he fell He had recently bought a new tin cup which was buckled onto his Haversack I took hold of it thinking I would take it for a Keepsake examining it a little closer found that a large minney ball had pased through his Haversack and went into his person I was told by the men that burried him that there was seven ball holes in his person there was clods of Blood on the ground where His lifes Blood had Ebbed away. His name was James Johnston from Hartwelville Mich. He was buried on the West side of the Wheatfield by a large Rock. The principle part of the dead was carried on stretchers to the woods west of the Wheatfield for interment. all the painess possible was taken in their burial trenches was dug and the bottom was neatly coverd with blankets and their remains was carefully an neatley layed side by side. blankets was torn into and made a roll to put under Each ones Head then blankets was spread over them and tucked down closely so no dirt could not tuch them. in some cases their Blody garments were removed and washed and dried on limbs of treas then Replased....

Could this be the rock, "on the West side of the Wheatfield," where James Johnston was so kindly laid to rest?

In all of the narratives I have ever read concerning the burials of Union or Confederate soldiers, this is the first mention of burial parties actually washing the dirty bloodstained clothes of the deceased then dressing the corpses for battlefield interment. It must have been a touching and heartbreaking scene, and the love and kindness shown by these unusual soldiers go far beyond the bounds of ordinary decency.

Second Lieutenant Franklin K. Garland, Company A, 61st New York Infantry, 1st Brigade, 1st Division, 2nd Corps

It is a rare occurrence when one may ascertain the exact spot on which a wounded or dying man lay for a time during the battle of Gettysburg or on any other battlefield for that matter. In the case of this twenty-one-year-old officer from Sherburne, New York, that is in fact possible, due to the recollections of another lieutenant of the regiment, Charles A. Fuller.

Lieutenant Fuller was wounded twice in Rose's wheatfield on July 2 at about 6 o'clock in the evening. After several hours there he was transported by ambulance to a field hospital at the Jacob Weikert farm on the Taneytown Road, a short distance to the rear. Here he related that,

> ...the noise of battle ceased and rumors began to circulate that the Rebs were defeated. I was again carried some distance and put down on the porch of a stone house that went about it on two or three sides. During the day the boys about me had occasionally poured water from their canteens on

to my wounds, [left leg and arm] which had soaked my clothing. I ached all over and a change of position almost in any form would have been a great relief, but the only movement I could make was to stir my right leg and arm. I had not been long on this stoop when Franklin G. Garland *[sic]* was brought and laid down near to me. We had grown up together from our baby days. A bullet had gone through his lungs, and every breath he took sent the air through the wound with a sickening rattle. I remember that they raised me up so that I could see him and I asked, "Are you badly wounded, Frank?" He replied, "Oh, yes!"

The present day veranda of the old Jacob Weikert house. Lt. F.K. Garland spent some painful and anxious hours here on another such wooden porch many years ago.

A few days later, Captain Willard Keech of the 61st sent a telegram to Garland's hometown at Sherburne with the words, "Garland mortally wounded; Fuller dangerously wounded; [Isaac] Plumb safe."

The lieutenant was soon moved from the porch of the Weikert farmhouse to the farm of a Mr. "J. Bair" or Bear where he died on July 4 and was buried there at the foot of a tree. This site is believed to have been near or along the Baltimore Pike, several miles south of the battlefield. His remains are now interred in the National Cemetery at Gettysburg.

 ## Corporal David C. Laird,
Company A, 4th Michigan Infantry,
2nd Brigade, 1st Division, 5th Corps

A delegate of the U.S. Christian Commission, Reverend Mr. R.J. Parvin, writing in 1868, commented on the above-named individual. This nineteen-year-old man from Adrian, Michigan had been wounded in the lumbar region of his body on July 2, again in the vicinity of the "wheatfield."

I found on the field a Michigan soldier named David Laird, and visited him regularly while I was at Gettysburg. One day, after writing home at his request, he told me of his early training, of his wandering from it, of his longing to return. We prayed, read and talked together, until at last the Spirit took possession of his heart. At first he was very much troubled because his wound—a serious one received while the regiment was falling back under orders—was in the back. I reassured him, and explained all the circumstances to his parents in my letter. I received answers from each of them, thanking me for my little ministries. But the mother's letter to her boy was perfect tenderness and love:

"DAVID, MY DARLING BOY: —What can I say to you, my son! my son? Oh, that I could see you! that I could minister to you! I think father will probably be with you soon. My dear one, you have done what you could to suppress this cruel rebellion. May God comfort you! You are still serving the country so dear to your heart. You have been for thirty months an active volunteer; now you are a suffering one. Still there is an army in which you may enlist,—the army of the Lord. All—all are welcome there. You will find kind friends who will keep us advised; and please request them to give us all the particulars of your situation. God comfort and sustain you, dear one, is your mother's prayer!"

His father also wrote, and mentioned the wound: "As to David's wound in his back, it need give him no uneasiness. None who know him will suppose it to be there on account of cowardice."

The weeks passed on; the pleasant September days arrived, but David was worse. His father came in time to see him die. When it was all over, I tried to comfort him for his loss, but he put the words kindly aside: "I don't need any comfort from man, for God has given me so much, in seeing the happy death of my boy, that I am perfectly content."

Corporal Laird was remembered, too, in the diary of Private Jacob Shenkel, 62nd Pennsylvania Infantry, who acted as a nurse for a time after the battle at Camp Letterman. He wrote:

"Monday, September 21:
got Pass to town telegraphed to Mr Laird to Come on His Son was very Low....

"Thursday, September 24:
Corporal David C. Laird Died about five o'clock this morning was Burried in Evening at five."

Laird was consigned to grave #23 in Section 8, of the hospital cemetery. Eventually he was permanently moved to the Michigan plot of the new Soldiers' National Cemetery at Gettysburg.

Private Rowland L. Ormsby, Company G, 64th New York Infantry, 4th Brigade, 1st Division, 2nd Corps

Mrs. Emily Bliss Thacher Souder of Philadelphia spent many weeks nursing the wounded at the Union Second Corps hospital, and later at the Letterman U.S. General Hospital near Gettysburg. Among her sad duties was the task of writing to relatives of soldiers who died in these hospitals. One such man was R.L. Ormsby, a twenty-one-year-old from Wellsville, New

York who had been wounded on July 2 in the right thigh. The bone was fractured by the bullet which resulted in the amputation of that limb at the upper third of the leg. Ormsby died on July 17 and was buried in a cornfield on the Jacob Schwartz farm three miles southwest of town. His body was later removed to the National Cemetery.

On two occasions, July 18 and July 22, Mrs. Souder mentions Private Ormsby in her letters home. Here is what she wrote to an unknown friend:

Gettysburg, July 18, 1863

Dear _____:

I was truly rejoiced to receive your letter with its inclosures. It is past eleven o'clock at night, and I have just finished a letter to the mother of a young man, of the New York 64th Volunteers, who died yesterday, and from whose head I cut a beautiful lock of black hair, which I enclosed with three oak leaves plucked from a branch which grew directly over his tent. We constantly witness heartbreaking scenes, but the Lord has endued us with strength to bear them.

On July 22, writing to "Friends," she identified the 64th man as Rowland Ormsby and added this line: "Two days after, the father came, but we did not see him."

This may at first appear to be a short and insignificant story. But think of it. Of the more than 5,000 Union soldiers who were killed or mortally wounded at Gettysburg, how many times could we say that even *these* few simple little things were done for them. How valuable those tiny relics must have been to the mother of Rowland. And how long they were surely held as cherished keepsakes in some sad Northern home. Perhaps as you read this, a lock of fading, musty black hair and a few hardened, withered leaves lay somewhere in New York in the back of a chest of drawers, or in an ancient trunk—all that remain of a life given at Gettysburg!

Private Charles F. Gardner,
Company H, 110th Pennsylvania Infantry,
3rd Brigade, 1st Division, 3d Corps

Two men were reported shot in the head and killed from this regiment on July 2 and buried on the south side of the George Rose farmhouse which had reposed for nearly forty-five years just west of Emmitsburg Road and south of Joseph Sherfy's peach orchard. Because the following description was so terrible in its sad beauty, I have chosen to use it even though I am unsure of the exact soldier in question. The other man was First Sergeant Joseph H. Care of Company A. Here is what the historian of the 116th Pennsylvania saw on that war-torn field.

In front and a little to the right stood the Rose Farm House and barn. Over the little valley in the immediate front one could see the enemy massed and preparing for another attack. The dead of the One Hundred and Tenth Pennsylvania Volunteers lay directly in front, on the ground which that command had vacated but a half hour before, and one young boy lay outstretched on a large rock with his musket still grasped in his hand, his pale, calm face upturned to the sunny sky, the warm blood still flowing from a hole in his forehead and running in a red stream over the gray stone. The young hero had just given his life for his country. A sweet, childish face it was, lips parted in a smile—those still lips on which the mother's kisses had so lately fallen, warm and tender. The writer never looked on a soldier slain without feeling that he gazed upon the relics of a saint; but the little boy lying there with his blood coloring the soil of his own State, and his young heart stilled forever, seemed more like an angel form than any of the others.

> "Somebody's watching and waiting for him,
> Yearning to hold him again to her heart;
> And there he lies with his blue eyes dim,
> And the smiling child-like lips apart.''

This rock may have been the one on which the blood of Private Gardner flowed so freely that hot July afternoon over 128 years ago.

Both Gardner and Care were later taken to the Soldiers' National Cemetery where they lie buried today. My belief that the dead young man was Gardner stems from the fact that the eyewitness did not mention the corpse wearing the chevrons of a first sergeant. Furthermore, I fail to see the lad described above as ever having had to discipline and drill a company of one hundred men at the time of the American Civil War. However, the reader will please kindly favor me with his or her judicious tolerance.

Private William L. Purbeck,
5th Massachusetts Light Artillery,
1st Volunteer Brigade, Artillery Reserve

When the 5th Massachusetts Battery went into the fight of July 2, a second time, just beyond the Abraham Trostle farm buildings, Corporal Benjamin Graham, commander of one of the guns, recollected:

> I ordered the piece to halt, and went into action...we stood...till sundown. It was here where little Purbeck was wounded.

The men moved the Gun in this manner: —Hayden No. 1, Purbeck 2, 5, 7, Kay 3 & 4, Shackley 6, Graham, Gunner.

We had not been in action long, when a shell from one of the reb batteries exploding on our right, struck one of General [Winfield S.] Hancock's aides-de-camp, and his horse; the horse falling on the officer. The officer was calling for help, and the horse was whinnying, as much as to say, "Help me, too," when little Purbeck, a good, smart boy, only 17, saw the man and horse down, and started to go over towards them, when he, too, got hit in the side with a piece of shell. He was taken to the rear and to the hospital, where he died that night, and as he was dying he uttered these words,—"Who will care for Mother now?" They suggested the song which became immensely popular.

As I understand it, he was a widow's son and his mother's only support. The words were written by a sergeant of the 22d Regiment, and the music by some man in Boston. There was not a braver boy in the army than Purbeck.

Private William Purbeck's military records state that he was shot in the abdomen. He was from Salem, Massachusetts. The song mentioned by Corporal Graham was indeed very well received during the Civil War. It was written by Charles C. Sawyer, and is so beautiful, and so sad that my eyes still water each time I read it. What a tender epitaph for any soldier "killed in action." The words follow:

> Why am I so weak and weary,
> See how faint my heated breath,
> All around to me seems darkness,
> Tell me, comrades, is this death?

> Ah! how well I know your answer;
> To my fate I meekly bow
> If you'll only tell me truly,
> Who will care for mother now?

> Soon with angels I'll be marching,
> With bright laurels on my brow.
> I have for my country fallen.
> Who will care for mother now?

> Who will comfort her in sorrow?
> Who will dry the falling tear,
> Gently smooth her wrinkled forehead?
> Who will whisper words of cheer?

> Even now I think I see her
> Kneeling, praying for me! how
> Can I leave her in her anguish?
> Who will care for mother now?

> Let this knapsack be my pillow,
> And my mantle be the sky;
> Hasten, comrades, to the battle,
> I will like a soldier die.

Soon with angels I'll be marching,
With bright laurels on my brow,
I have for my country fallen,
Who will care for mother now?

Private John Buckley, Company B, 140th Pennsylvania Infantry, 3rd Brigade, 1st Division, 2nd Corps

Lieutenant James J. Purman won the Congressional Medal of Honor for his brave actions during the Battle of Gettysburg. He was wounded twice on July 2, and later married a local woman, Mary Witherow, who had nursed him back to health in her family's house. The following is Purman's account of meeting Private Buckley on that fateful day.

On the afternoon of July 2, 1863, my brigade had charged across the historic "wheatfield" and driven the enemy into the woods beyond. In turn we were driven back, our ranks broken up in the woods and among the rocks. When we emerged from the woods and were about to retreat across the wheatfield, the only man of my company whom I could see was Orderly Sgt. J.M. Pipes. At this moment we came across a comrade whom I did not know, badly wounded in the legs. He cried out, "Comrades, carry me off!" I replied that we could not do that as the enemy was too close upon us, but immediately noticed two rocks nearly suitable for protection from the enemy's fire, and said to the orderly sgt., "Come help me and we will put him between these rocks." With the assistance of the sgt., I carried him and placed him between these rocks in an apparent place of safety. I remained with him long enough to straighten out his limbs and take his hand and say goodbye. But this delay of a few minutes caused the enemy to gain upon me so much that it proved fatal to my intention of crossing the wheatfield and reaching our reserves on the opposite side. Within a few yards of me the enemy called out "Halt, you damned Yankee, halt!" I did not obey this command and, in consequence, a few moments later received a gunshot in my left leg below the knee, crushing both bones, and fell instantly to the ground, the enemy charging over me. Unable to crawl off, I lay on the field all night and the next day, between the fires of both armies....Since the war I have ascertained that the unknown comrade whose life I tried to save was John Buckley, Co. B of my own regiment, and that he died from loss of blood and exposure before help could reach him.

Buckley was soon buried near the farmhouse of either George or John Weikert, both northeast of the wheatfield area. Fortunately, his remains were later reinterred to the Pennsylvania plot of the National Cemetery.

First Lieutenant Horatio F. Lewis, Company D, 145th Pennsylvania Infantry, 4th Brigade, 1st Division, 2nd Corps

Chaplain John Stuckenberg was a twenty-eight-year-old Lutheran minister

51

who kept a diary of his service with the 145th Pennsylvania. On July 7 he visited the field hospital of his division to bring bread, cakes, butter and eggs to the wounded of the regiment. There he found,

> ...Lt. [George H.] Finch was dead...& most of the others of our regt. were doing well. Lt. Lewis had his leg amputated. He looked feeble & sallow, suffered a great deal had been lying on the field till a rebel for 25 dolls. brought him to a house to their rear, but [they] stole his water canteen, his money about 80 dolls. et cet. and [he] could not sleep. He has since then died. He was a noble young man, knew a good deal about military affairs and made a good officer. He was brave, ambitious and hopeful. There was an innocence and simplicity about him, which were well calculated to gain one's affection. His loss is felt severely by us all. We loved him, we admired him. He is one of the many truly noble sacrifices given to our country. He was calm and resigned when I saw him, and frequently, I was told, was found praying. The thought of his death greatly saddens me, for I loved him and had great hopes for him. Never shall I forget how willingly he once received my reproofs for what turned out to be a sham duel.

Lieutenant Finch had been wounded near or in the area of Rose's wheatfield on the afternoon of July 2. His death took place on July 6, 1863, at the Jacob Schwartz farm which was serving as the main field hospital of the Second Army Corps. The lieutenant was initially buried in "Yard D," a cornfield used as one of the hospital's cemeteries. He now rests peacefully in the National Cemetery at Gettysburg.

 ### Private William Chamberlain, Company I, 141st Pennsylvania Infantry, 1st Brigade, 1st Division, 3rd Corps

Sergeant John Bloodgood took time on July 4, 1863 to look over the recent field of battle, especially in the area of the so-called "Valley of Death" between Houck's Ridge and Little Round Top. He was searching for his missing tentmate, Oliver Morse, whose body was never found. Later on that day Bloodgood walked to a field hospital to find and visit his mangled and battered friends. His memoir of that trip is published here.

> I next went to our Third Corps hospital to see some of our boys who had been wounded. Just as I arrived an attendant was carrying out a wheelbarrow load of bare arms and legs which the surgeons had just been amputating. It was the most horrid sight I had yet witnessed, and I involuntarily turned away from it. I found several of our company here more or less severely wounded. One young man, William Chamberlain, lay on a stretcher totally unconscious, his life rapidly ebbing away. I wrote a note to his father, who resided at Wysox, Pa., informing him of his son's condition. The poor fellow lingered till Tuesday, the 7th, when he quietly breathed his last. His remains were taken home by some of his neighbors who were visiting the battlefield, and were committed to rest amid the green hills of his own native State....

Federal military service records do not indicate where Chamberlain was shot or otherwise injured, only that he died on the tenth of July. The deplorable wound he received must surely have come from a bullet fired by a South Carolina or Mississippi infantryman near Sherfy's peach orchard late on July 2. For someone living near Wysox, Pennsylvania, it would be an interesting quest to attempt to locate Private Chamberlain's present resting place.

Second Lieutenant Benjamin R. Wright, Company A, 26th Pennsylvania Infantry, 1st Brigade, 2nd Division, 3rd Corps

Baffling circumstances surround the short but appealing story of this young Philadelphian. His military record denotes that he was killed outright on July 2 when the 26th lost 213 of its 365 men fighting near the peach orchard on July 2, south of Gettysburg. This brave regiment lost fifty-six men killed or mortally wounded on that awful afternoon along the Emmitsburg Road.

Nothing exceptional could be found about Lieutenant Wright, until this most unusual encounter transpired. A soldier of the 51st Pennsylvania on furlough from his unit visited the battlefield from July 7 through the 10th. On the last day of his visit this man, John B. Linn, wrote in his diary:

> Friday July 10, 1863....
>
> Sick of hospitals and tired of my dirty clothes I got a chance to ride to Carlisle with Zimmerman, Ed Stock and others, came by way of Petersburg [York Springs] where I met Jim Coburn. Bridges were swept away by the breaking of Mountain Creek dam. Passed on the road the corpse of Lieut. Wright of the 26 Penna. At Papertown [Mt. Holly Springs] or near it in the gap we had a great deal of trouble fording. Reached Carlisle about 7 at night.

The question is obvious: Why was Wright's body here, in or near the Mt. Holly gap, twenty-one miles north of Gettysburg? Were there people with the corpse? Had his friends or family exhumed the body and were trying to get it home to the Philadelphia area? The answers may never be known, but the mystery is an intriguing one, and I, for one, regret that I am unable to write a proper end to this puzzling situation.

Sergeant William S. Jordan, Company G, 20th Maine Infantry, 3rd Brigade, 1st Division, 5th Corps

One of the many delegates working with the U.S. Christian Commission was attending to the wounded at the Union Army's Fifth Corps hospital when he discovered a young man dangerously ill from the effects of a gunshot wound. He was pale and sinking fast and the delegate conjectured that it needed but one look to see that he could not survive. I inquired his name. "Wm. J_____," was the only answer that he had strength to make audible. I had several of the little books in my hand which have been prepared for the soldiers, and I placed these by his pillow. He reached out his feeble hand, and looking them over picked out one with the title "Welcome to Jesus," printed in gold on a purple cover, and whispered to me to place that on the window-sill before him, upright, so that he could see those words without turning his head. I did so.

The surgeon came to dress his wounds. The patient, evidently near his end, and almost without breath for speaking, held out his hand to thank me, and I left him. That night he died. The last comforting message he had was, as I have reason to believe, the soul-cheering one, "Welcome to Jesus." But what a message was that! Thanks, many thanks, to the liberal people who sustain me and my associates in furnishing such means for comforting the departing soul in such an hour.

Jordan expired on July 24 from a bullet wound through his left lung. He was decently buried on the farm of John Trostle a short distance from the farmhouse of Michael Fiscel, the building in which he may have died. Both of these farms served as hospitals for the Fifth and Sixth Corps after the Battle of Gettysburg, and are about three miles south of town. Sergeant Jordan was soon moved to the National Cemetery where his permanent grave is marked clearly in the Maine state plot.

Private Alvin L. Greenlee,
Company F, 140th Pennsylvania Infantry,
3rd Brigade, 1st Division, 2nd Corps

On July 2, Private Greenlee was wounded very seriously through the thigh by a Minie' ball which fractured the bone. He was found and carried to one of the field hospitals of the Second Corps. A few weeks after the battle he was transported to Camp Letterman General Hospital. Here Greenlee was first visited by his mother who had the woeful duty of remaining by his side until he took his final breath on August 3. During her lonely vigil Mrs. Greenlee boarded with the Gettysburg family of James Pierce who lived on the southwest corner of Baltimore and Breckenridge Streets. Years later, Pierce's daughter, Matilda, recounted her sad ordeal.

The friends and relatives who came to minister to the wounded were, on account of the crowded condition of the hotels, compelled to ask accommodations from private citizens. In this manner quite a number were taken into our home. Most of their time was spent at the hospital, some coming back to us in the evening, and leaving as soon as possible the next morning.

I was frequently invited to accompany these visitors, and in this way often found myself by the bedside of the wounded.

One lady who was stopping at our house, I remember in particular; a Mrs. Greenly [sic]. Her son lay suffering at the hospital, and in company we frequently visited him.

One day when he was very low it was concluded that by amputating his limb his life might be spared. After the operation had been performed her son sank rapidly. At last came the words: "Mother! Dear Mother!—Good bye!—Good!—Mother!" —and all was over. Her darling boy lay before her in the embrace of death; but a mother's tender love had traced a peaceful smile upon his countenance. As the life went out from that racked body hope and joy forsook that fond mother's heart.

Oh! that sad face and bleeding spirit, as she bade us farewell to follow the coffined remains to her far off home.

Who will dare to say that with such sacrifices upon our country's altar our national inheritance is not sacredly precious?

I shall never forget the anxious suspense of that mother. Whilst absent from her loved one, even for a few hours, her spirit knew no rest, and as soon as possible she would hurry back.

Private James H. McCleary,
Battery B, 1st Pennsylvania Reserve Artillery,
Artillery Brigade, 1st Corps

At about four o'clock p.m. on July 2, a Confederate battery of four 20-pounder and six 10-pounder Parrotts positioned in a wheatfield 1,300 yards east of Cemetery Hill, opened fire on Union batteries of the First Corps Artillery Brigade commanded by Colonel Charles Wainwright. During this engagement of one-and-one-half hours, Colonel Wainwright noted the shocking death of an artilleryman who was very likely James McCleary, who had lived in Lawrence County, Pennsylvania. In his diary account of July 2, the colonel transcribed:

....So soon as the shell burst [among the gun crew] I jumped from the wall, and told [Captain James H.] Cooper to put on another detachment, that General [Adelbert] Ames would let some of his men carry off the wounded; not a murmur was uttered, but five other men at once took place over their dead and wounded comrades, and fired before they could be removed. I was very proud of it. The man who was so badly blown to pieces lost his right hand, his left arm at the shoulder, and his ribs so broken open that you could see right into him; he was removed to the well, just inside the cemetery gates, and died there. Cooper came to me and asked permission for [the wounded man's] brother, who was their bugler, to go and remain with him while he lived. The bugler, who had nothing to do, would not go sixty or seventy yards from his battery to see his brother in his last moments without permission, nor would his captain give the permission without asking mine. Yet were they in camp, hardly a man in the battery but would go off for all day without permission to see a well brother, and Cooper would think it all right.

The records of the battery indicate that McCleary was also wounded in both legs and was buried on the east side of the Evergreen Cemetery. Today, the well where Private McCleary spent his remaining few moments of life with his brother is easily visited behind the brick "gatehouse" along the Baltimore turnpike on Cemetery Hill.

Private Solan L. Cornell,
Company A, 17th United States Infantry,
2nd Brigade, 2nd Division, 5th Corps

Near the close of the day on July 2, during the extremely intense fighting which took place between the base of Little Round Top and Rose's twenty-five acre wheatfield, a soldier named J.P. Hackett witnessed the tragic death of a close companion. Fifty-two years afterwards he could still describe the wild scene.

Then there came to [the Confederates] fresh reinforcements, and we were almost overpowered. Sergeant Sanborn standing almost elbow-touch with me, received a ball in his shoulder, and our Captain [Dudley H.] (Chase), seeing it, said "Hackett, guide left on Company D." which brought me in touch with Capt. [William J.] Moorhead. Then a bullet struck him below the knee and he fell forward, saying as cooly as if it were only a snowfall, "Go on, boys." Then Private Cornell was shot thru the body near the waistline. He was a dear friend of mine, and as he fell he threw his arms around my neck, saying, "Oh, Hackett, I am killed."

I lifted him in my arms and carried him back and laid him tenderly down. He begged me not to leave him, but Lieut. [Robert P.] Wilson said kindly: "You must take your place in the ranks."

And I did. For a few minutes I was completely rattled. Then as I picked up my gun, I thought vengeance is mine, and I will repay, and I at least tried to repay with a vengeance. While in line of battle on Round Top [earlier in the day] I, in jubilation over the coming conflict, said to Cornell: "What hotel will you put up in tonight?"

He answered: "I hope not in hell," and I looked at the poor boy, and he was deathly pale, although there was no lack of firmness in his step, and I know now that he must have had a premonition of death.

Private Cornell, twenty-one years old, was a "wood turner" before the war, who had been born in Knox, Ohio. He is buried today in the U.S. Regulars section of the National Cemetery in Gettysburg. When his corpse was removed to that government cemetery, the burial squad found two photographs, two knives, and two gun wrenches with the remains. Though pale and fearful, Cornell had met the enemies of his country with firmness and courage. Certainly, that is all that needs to be said.

Sergeant Major Charles Ward,
32nd Massachusetts Infantry, 2nd Brigade,
1st Division, 5th Corps

While fighting on Thursday, the Second day of July just southwest of the "wheatfield" or "maelstrom of death" as it has sometimes been designated, Lieutenant Colonel Luther Stephenson, Jr. was badly wounded in the face. His encounter with Sergeant Major Ward was graphically recalled almost twenty years later.

On the 3d of July the wounded of the 5th corps were taken from the barns and other buildings in the immediate vicinity of the battle field, where they had been placed during the progress of the fight, to a large grove about two miles distant.

The trains containing hospital supplies and tents had not arrived, and the wounded were placed under little shelter-tents, such as the soldiers carried with them upon the march. We lay on the bare ground without even straw for our beds, and he who obtained a knapsack for a pillow deemed himself fortunate.

Just at night the attendants brought to the place where I was lying, a young soldier of the 32d and laid him beside me. It was Charles Ward of Newton. I remembered him well as one of the youngest of the Regiment, one whose purity of character, and attention to duty had won the esteem and love of all who knew him. The attendants placed him in the tent, furnished us with canteens of water, and left us for the night, for alas, there were thousands of wounded men to be cared for, and but little time could be spared for any one. My young companion had been wounded by a ball passing through his lungs, and it was with difficulty he could breathe while lying down. To relieve him, I laid flat on my back, putting up my knees, against which he leaned in a sitting posture. All night long we remained in this position, and a painful weary night it was. At intervals we would catch a few moments of sleep; then waking, wet our wounds with water from the canteens, try to converse, and then again to sleep. So we wore away the night, longing for the light to come.

No one came near us; we heard far away the dropping fire of musketry on the picket lines, the occasional booming of the cannon, and the groans wrung from the lips of hundreds of wounded men around us. My young friend knew that he must die; never again to hear the familiar voices of home, never to feel a mother's kiss, away from brothers, sisters, and friends; yet as we talked he told me that he did not for a moment regret the course he had taken in enlisting in the war of the Union, but that he was ready, willing to die, contented in the thought that his life was given in the performance of his duty to his country.

Charles Ward, aged twenty, lingered until July 9 when he died at the Third Division hospital of the Fifth Corps somewhere near or on the Michael Fiscel farm. I am saddened to say that I am unable to report to the reader the grave site of this fine and dedicated young man.

Colonel Charles F. Taylor, 42nd Pennsylvania Infantry, 1st Brigade, 3rd Division, 5th Corps

Charles Taylor was born in West Chester, Pennsylvania in 1840 and later attended the University of Michigan. He was commissioned captain of Co. H at the outset of the Civil War, rising to the rank of Colonel by 1863. On July 2 in the charge made by the Pennsylvania Reserves from the base of Little Round Top to a woods just east of that by now, well-known wheatfield, Taylor was struck by a bullet near the heart and died soon afterwards. He was believed to be the youngest colonel serving in the Union ranks at Gettysburg. The circumstances of his death were described as follows.

Just after the line halted we received a heavy volley from our right-center. Colonel Taylor with two other officers and fifteen or twenty men were on that part of the line at the time. Quickly facing to the left they discovered, but a short distance away, two hundred or three hundred rebels partly hidden by the timber. An officer promptly demanded their surrender when nearly every man in their line threw down his arms. Just then a Confederate in the rear of their line sang out with an oath, "I'll never surrender to a corporal's guard." The rebels again grasped their arms when Lieutenant [J. Elliott] Kratzer called out to the Bucktails, "Tree every man of you," and, jumping behind a tree near him, he turned to Colonel Taylor, who was near by, and urged him to hurry. Just as the colonel laid his hand on Lieutenant Kratzer's shoulder, and was in the act of stepping under shelter of the tree, a rebel sharpshooter sent a bullet through his heart—when our brave and beloved commander died without speaking a word....

Colonel Charles Frederick Taylor,
42nd Pennsylvania Infantry.

A letter written by another member of the regiment adds more to the somber story:

On Picket near Sharpsburg & Hagerstown Rd.
Saturday July 11th, 1863

Miss Annie Taylor,

Yours of the 6th is just received. You ask concerning the fall of a brother. I am very sorry that what little information I had was not sent immediately but relying on others more capable is my excuse.

He fell at (I suppose about 6 o'clock) in the extreme front—he was urging the men forward [and] about the last words he spoke before he fell were to a rebel reg't not over fifty yards in front of us. He called to them to hault [sic] & surrender. He fell, I was with him in an instant—he told me where he was wounded & asked for water   after taking a little water—blood began to come from his mouth & he seemed to want to say something. All I could understand was "Mum" "Mum." I do not think that he lasted over two minutes. I helped to carry him off the field & took charge of what few things he had about him, which things I afterwards turned over to Capt. [John] Yerkes.

Lieut. [George] Ludlow, Co. E of this reg't was with the body & told me he would have it sent home. So I went back to the front & next day found that Lieut. Ludlow had taken the body to a hosp. & there left it—when two of our boys Richard West, [and] W[illiam] T. Gause found it & did all they could under the circumstances.

Believing I have told you all as best I could, I remain very respectfully
Your most obedient servt.
Aaron Baker

Taylor's brother, Bayard, said of him: "Nobody knows how dear Fred was to me; through him I knew what a brother's love meant. I had brighter hopes for him than myself: he was better and nobler than I."

Colonel Taylor's body was eventually interred in Longwood Cemetery near his home. A granite marker, dedicated in 1905, which points out the spot where he fell is now in place on the Gettysburg battlefield.

Second Lieutenant Robert E. Evans, Company C, 108th New York Infantry, 2nd Brigade, 3rd Division, 2nd Corps

The 108th New York, recruited around Rochester in August 1862, found itself supporting Woodruff's Battery I, 1st U.S. Artillery in an area known as Ziegler's Grove on Cemetery Ridge before sunset on the evening of July 2. One of the surgeons of the regiment was there, as the Confederate artillery pounded the position held by Lieutenant George A. Woodruff and the 108th which was supporting it. The doctor stated that it

was impossible to escape the continual shower of missiles aimed at the battery. While we lay thus, a shell with its fuze burning passed between the heads of myself and Col. [Francis E.] Pierce—the burning fuze slightly singing my left whisker as it passed....In a short time shrieks and groans were heard around us...one [man] I saw whose face was partially swept away by a shell. He clung to his gun for a few moments uttering unearthly screams....One of our men was rolling on the ground in agony—a piece of shell having struck him on the hip. Lieut. [A.D.J.] McDonald sprang to his feet with a cry, a ball having passed through his shoulder. Lieut. Evans rolled over in the agonies of death, shot in the brain. Myself and orderly Charles Dickson now had to get to our feet....we removed the wounded man [Evans] a few yards in the rear where by stooping low behind a low heap of field— boulders there was some slight shelter from the storm. Here I examined his wound and found the bullet had struck just in front of the ear and passed out behind, tearing up one of the most vital points of the brain. He expired on my knee in about twenty minutes. It was said he was from Toronto.

Another who saw the wounding of Evans was Lieutenant Theron E. Parsons of the 108th. He related that Lieutenant Evans, "was shot through the head, the ball entering his ear and coming out, making two holes within two inches of each other. Poor fellow! He was a good man, and he rests peacefully.''

Robert Evans was twenty-nine at the time of his death and had been a resident of Rochester, New York.

Private Cyrus Plumer,
Company H, 62nd Pennsylvania Infantry,
2nd Brigade, 1st Division, 5th Corps

There is a small bright spot in the history of Cyrus Plumer which will be illuminated shortly—a possible good end to one more tragedy of the Battle of Gettysburg.

Plumer, from Allegheny County, Pennsylvania, enlisted in the summer of 1861 along with his brother, Daniel, who succumbed to disease before the setting in of winter that same year.

Cyrus Plumer fought safely through several battles prior to Gettysburg, and in one, Chancellorsville, he wrote home that, "One ball passed through my hair, but did not hurt me."

It was on July 2, 1863, however, that Plumer's luck ran out. Defending against a Confederate attack just southwest of the "wheatfield" at about 5:00 p.m. he was mortally wounded by a musket ball which entered his body in the region of the loins. Another source, oddly, maintains that the shot hit him in the head. In any event, he was very seriously hurt, and his lieutenant, John D. Sauters said later:

"Our Regt. was ordered to fall back a short distance, and as Cyrus was a general favorite in the company, several of his comrades exerted themselves to get him off the field, in which they succeeded...."

Plumer must have lived for a short time, because he was transported to the field hospital of the Fifth Corps, about two miles southeast of the place he was wounded. He eventually died there sometime that evening. A small cemetery had been established on the farmer's property and Plumer was interred in it, a simple headboard marking the grave. In the months after the battle, a local farmer, Mr. John G. Frey, recorded the grave and headboard as still in place.

David Neville of Export, Pennsylvania has done extensive research on Plumer. I shall let Mr. Neville continue the story:

> For many years the family of Cyrus Plumer believed he was buried in the National Cemetery; however, a review of the grave sites fails to reveal a grave for Private Plumer. Therefore, it must be assumed that he was buried in the Pennsylvania section as an "Unknown." Why the family believed he was buried there; especially if he were buried as an "Unknown," and where they got this information is not known and remains a mystery.
>
> Now 128 years after his death new evidence and research has revealed the possible grave site of Private Plumer. All 526 Pennsylvania graves were

carefully examined, with only one yielding the necessary information qualifying it as his possible burial site. The grave placed under scrutiny was D-33 in the Pennsylvania Section, marked "Unknown." The following convincing evidence has been presented.

During the war Cyrus Plumer corresponded frequently with his sister Mary Ann, with some of his letters to her existing to this day. When the individual buried in D-33 was disinterred for burial in the National Cemetery he was found with two items on his body, namely books and two letters from a "Mary Ann." Further study of the graves preceding as well as following D-33, reveal that all of these men were identified as members of First Division, Fifth Corps units; the same division that Plumer belonged to. This suggests that all of these deceased soldiers were removed from the same Cemetery that Plumer was buried in and were thus buried as a group.

Could this previously unknown grave be the final resting place of Private Cyrus Plumer?...

Private Cyrus Plumer,
62nd Pennsylvania Infantry.

It must be assumed that some family member eventually ventured to Adams County to locate Plumer's grave site. And ironically, a soldier of the 62nd Pennsylvania wrote in his diary on Wednesday, October 21, 1863 from Camp Letterman, where he was still detailed as a nurse: "Calvin P. Lawrence and James Hudler Left to go to Hospital in Baltimore. Had Introduction to Steward Knowles and His wife also to Miss Plummer"

Was "Miss Plummer" the sister of Cyrus, Mary Ann Plumer? Perhaps we shall never know the answers to any of the questions presented here. But it would be quite comforting to believe that the concern and hard work shown by present day historian David Neville, may have brought about a delayed discovery and happy ending to one minute chapter of the history of this renowned battle.

Colonel Edward E. Cross,
5th New Hampshire Infantry, 1st Brigade,
1st Division, 2nd Corps

During the Gettysburg Campaign and subsequent to his death, Colonel Cross was acting brigade commander of the 1st Brigade in General John Caldwell's Division. Prior to this, as colonel of the 5th New Hampshire, he had made a reputation as a strict disciplinarian, often reacting to a breach of military rules in a seemingly petty, tyrannical way. This situation in the brigade had become to some, untenable. On the march to Gettysburg the final insult came when Cross assigned Colonel H.B. McKeen of the 81st Pennsylvania to command the 148th Pennsylvania, in place of Lieutenant Colonel Robert McFarlane. The act was described by a member of the 148th as, "wholly unjustifiable, the culmination of a series of insults and indignities, which...he had inflicted on the Regiment."

Colonel Edward E. Cross,
5th New Hampshire Infantry.

At approximately six o'clock p.m. on July 2 Colonel Cross was situated a few hundred yards west of Little Round Top, and a little east of the "wheatfield." While directing the movements of his brigade, Cross was struck in the abdomen by a Minie' ball, near the center of the body, which passed through and out near the spine. The spot on the battlefield where he fell is today marked by the monument of the 5th New Hampshire Infantry. A few rods south of this site is a large boulder, surmounted by a smaller rock. A witness at the scene stated that a rebel soldier had sighted his rifle from atop this boulder, killing the colonel. Only moments passed until a sergeant of the 5th circled around to the side of the Confederate's position and shot him to death. A member of the regiment, told what occurred next:

> Thus wounded he was carried about one mile to a locality directly in the rear of the right wing of the army, near Culp's hill, into the midst of a wheatfield. The crop had just been cut and bound into sheaves. A good number of these were gathered by his attendants and a comfortable bed was form-

ed, upon which the noble form of the dying hero and patriot was tenderly laid. The gloom of a deep darkness covered all. Some camp-fires crackled and glimmered, flashed and cast weird shadows around the group of friends and attendants. Now and then a shell went screeching across the sky, bursting with a sudden flash and stunning report. Many of his regiment, men who had followed him in a score of battles, were around. His brother, Major [Richard E.] Cross, was bending low by his side; his surgeon, Major J.W. Bucknam, rendered skillful medical aid and friendly comfort. Assistant-Surgeon [William] Child silently watched the colonel whom he so much admired and respected. Standing near by were the officers and men who had so often followed him into battle. All faces were sad, all hearts were sorrowful. The dying warrior had a kind word for all. To his officers and men he sent messages of love, of respect, of encouragement. To his brother he gave messages of love to his sisters and brothers, and with tears and sighs urged his brother to care for the mother and to convey to her his tenderest regard and love. Shells were bursting near; spiteful picket firing was in every direction. Life was drawing to an end in that noble form. He constantly murmured, "My brave men." In pain he lived on another hour and still another, until at 12:30 midnight that brave spirit went out on the great battle-field.

An officer of the 5th, Thomas L. Livermore, upon hearing of the wounding of Cross, attempted to locate him during the night of July 2. It was not until after midnight when he found the site. It was:

...a little dell, possibly one through which a little stream ran, between the Taneytown road and the Baltimore road, and from a quarter to half a mile from my [ambulance] park going toward Gettysburg. Here under the shelter of some boulders lay a large number of our wounded and dead who had been brought from the field. They lay upon the ground covered with their blankets, and the living were nearly all silent, having fallen asleep from fatigue. I picked my way among their prostrate forms to the spot where the colonel lay, and inquiring of an officer of my regiment, whom I saw, which was the colonel, he pointed him out to me, indicating that he was dead. I went to him and turned his blanket back from his face, and saw it was true that he was dead. The moonlight or starlight enabled me to see his features distinctly. They were placid and exceedingly lifelike, and it was hard to persuade myself that the flush of life had gone from them. His lofty forehead was smooth, his long, silky beard lay upon his breast undisheveled, and he looked more as he would if he slept than seemed possible. I was told that he had called those of his regiment who were about him and told them that he did not regret death, except that he had hoped to see the rebellion suppressed; that he hoped they would be good soldiers and keep up the discipline and good conduct of the regiment. He sent for various members of the regiment, myself included, and also my little [servant] boy Charlie, to bid us farewell.

Sitting beside the colonel listening to what the officer told me about him at midnight, surrounded by many wounded, was a sad experience and one which can never forsake my memory; among the other circumstances which

I recall is this, that lying close by us was a lieutenant of the 2d New Hampshire Volunteers mortally wounded (I think his name was [Charles W.] Patch), and it was a mournful thing to think of his dying there, not only away from home, but away from those of his own regiment who might have cared for him.

Sometime during the early hours of July 3, 1863, everyone near to or attending to the corpse of Colonel Cross must have wandered off to their duties, or had fallen asleep. One group which was not asleep however, was a small detail of "pioneers" led by Sergeant T.P. Meyers of the 148th Pennsylvania who had been sent forth into the various hospitals to bury bodies as they could be found. Working by the light of a few sperm candles in an, "open air field hospital, behind a rocky bluff on Rock Creek, one mile to our right rear...."

Colonel Cross was shot from a position near here. He fell where the 5th N.H. monument now stands in the background.

Meyers reported: "Some of my men carried out the dead and laid them in rows, heads all one way, and one against the other. About the third man carried out was the tyrant commander of our Brigade, Colonel Cross, of the 5th New Hampshire Regiment, killed in the woods near the wheat field. We did not bury him."

Colonel Cross' body was embalmed and sent home, accompanied by Captain W.A. Crafts, to Lancaster, New Hampshire, where it arrived on July 7. The funeral ceremonies were held at his family homestead on July 9; the casket, draped with a U.S. flag, on which rested his sword and cap, stood on the long low piazza of the house. The burial took place amid a host of friends and relatives who had known him from boyhood.

Edward E. Cross' story cannot end here, without mentioning the strange and strong premonition he seemed to possess concerning what he believed would be his forthcoming death.

On Sunday the 28th of June while enroute to Pennsylvania with the Army of the Potomac, Cross told one of his staff officers, Lieutenant Charles A.

Hale, in speaking of the expected battle, "It will be my last battle." Hale said the sentence was given in a grave, decided way, which shocked the young officer. A few seconds later Cross told Hale:

"Mr. Hale, I wish you to attend to my books and papers. That private box of mine in the headquarters wagon—you helped me to re-pack it the other day. After the campaign is over, get it at once, dry the contents if damp and then turn it over to my brother Richard."

Lieutenant Hale says too that on July 2 while nearing the battlefield, Cross again repeated, in a serious, firm way, "Mr. Hale: attend to that box of mine at the first opportunity."

Somewhat later Lieutenant Hale was called on to perform a rueful duty. He recounted:

> Presently, stopping short near where I was standing, he drew out from an inside pocket a large, new, black silk handkerchief. Arranging it in folds on his lifted knee, then handing me his hat to hold, he quickly swathed his head with it in turban fashion, tying the two ends behind. We had seen him do this on other fields with a red bandana and it then amused me somewhat, but under the peculiar circumstances of the few days previous the black handkerchief was appalling. Again he took off his hat, saying, "Please tie it tighter, Mr. Hale." My hands were trembling as I picked at the knot. "Draw it tighter still," he said impatiently, and finally I adjusted it to suit him.

A few moments passed and General W.S. Hancock, commanding the Second Corps rode up to where Cross was standing, holding his horse's head. Hancock called out: "Colonel Cross, this day will bring you a star." The colonel gravely shook his head and replied: "No General, this is my last battle."

And finally, Surgeon William Child of the 5th had a similar morbid experience to that of Charles Hale. He revealed that while the regiment was halted and the Second Corps was being massed for attack, he caught a glimpse of the colonel, who,

> ...gave to [my] care a massive gold ring, some valuable papers, a pocket book, and some other valuables. He said, "Good-by! It will be an awful day. Take care of yourself, I must go into the fight, but I fear I shall be killed. Good-by!"...he saluted and passed on to death and glory.

Major Israel P. Spalding, 141st Pennsylvania Infantry, 1st Brigade, 1st Division, 3rd Corps

Israel Putnam Spalding was born in Athens, Pennsylvania on January 22, 1825. He was engaged in farming and business with his father, Robert Spalding at the time of his enlistment in 1862. His spouse was Ruth E. Cooley whom he had married in December of 1852.

At the formation of the regiment, Spalding was elected major and grew into a good officer who had the respect and confidence of his men and his

Major Israel P. Spalding,
141st Pennsylvania Infantry.

superiors. In a last letter, written shortly before the Battle of Gettysburg, he epitomized his beliefs: "The enemy are now in my native state and I shall not fail in my duty to the flag we follow nor disgrace the uniform I wear."

In 1885, the historian of the 141st commented on the final days of Major Spalding's life, a life stripped from him on July 2 near a peach orchard two miles south of Gettysburg:

....As has been related he was twice wounded, one ball striking his thigh, and as he was being helped from the field another broke his ankle, and he was left in the hands of the enemy. All night he lay upon the battlefield, amid the dead, the dying, and the wounded, entirely helpless from his wounds which were indescribably painful. The next day Colonel [Benjamin G.] Humphreys, of the Eighteenth [21st] Mississippi Regiment, who held the ground, ordered him carried to the rear where a surgeon dressed his wounds and set a pail of water to keep the bandages wet. The soldiers of the enemy treated him very kindly. On Sunday the ankle was found so badly shattered that the leg was amputated below the knee. A week was spent in loneliness and pain. The enemy had been driven back and friends were ministering to his wants, but they were strangers. On the 10th he writes in his diary, "I was gratified to-day more than I can express, by the sight of a familiar face, the first I have seen since I was hurt. It was James McFarlane. God only knows, how much good it did me to see him. He was looking for me and brought several little things that were very acceptable. I shall not soon forget his kindness."

The next day his brother Hanson, Dr. Ladd and others from about Towanda reached the field, and he was lovingly and faithfully ministered to until his death, which occurred Tuesday, July 28th, in the thirty-ninth year of his age, leaving a wife, with two sons and a daughter.

His remains were brought to Wysox, where, on Sunday, August 2d, a large concourse of citizens assembled with sympathizing hearts while the last rites were solemnized, and there, in the churchyard cemetery, his soldier comrades entombed that form which in life had stood with them in the field of battle strife.

> *"There are paleness and weeping and sighs below;*
> *For our faith is faint and our tears will flow,*
> *But the harps of Heaven are ringing;*
> *Glad tidings come to greet him;*
> *And hymns of joy are singing,*
> *While old friends press to meet him."*

Captain Robert M. Forster, Company C, 148th Pennsylvania Infantry, 1st Brigade, 1st Division, 2nd Corps

Another soldier who fought and died in the tangled and bloody "wheatfield" on that sultry afternoon of July 2 was Robert Forster, described as "an able officer, of fine intelligence....a strict and excellent disciplinarian, prompt and energetic in the performance of every duty. He attended faithfully to the interests of his company, and always took great pride in seeing it in good condition."

On July 6, 1863, R.H. Forster, a captain of Company A, 148th Pennsylvania, and a kinsman of our subject, wrote to Mark Halfpenny, Esq.:

> It is with feelings of the most profound sorrow that I take this, the very first spare moment, to give you the sad intelligence of the death of your brother-in-law, Capt. Robert M. Forster, who fell, while gallantly leading his company into the action of Thursday evening near Gettysburg, pierced through the head with a musket ball. His death was, of course, instantaneous. His body was brought from the field and now lies buried on the farm of Mr. Jacob Himmelbach *[sic]*, about one mile from Gettysburg, and is marked. I visited the spot myself, in order that I might be able to render you any assistance in my power to recovering it at some future time. You will, of course, convey this sad and heartrending news to his mother.

Captain Robert M. Forster,
148th Pennsylvania Infantry.

I will not attempt to offer any vain words of consolation of my own to hearts that I know will be almost over-powered with grief and sorrow at the receipt of the sad intelligence this letter bears. I can only add that we all feel that the Regiment has lost one of its bravest and most efficient officers, while, for myself personally, I am fully conscious that as a valued friend and camp companion his place will never be filled.

R.H. Forster had visited the field hospital at the Hummelbaugh farm on the night of July 2. While there he noticed so many amputated limbs piled up and scattered outside a window of the small house that it was difficult not to tread on them as he searched for Robert.

Interestingly, a member of the 51st Pennsylvania, John B. Linn, mentioned earlier, recorded this in his diary on Thursday, July 9, 1863. "....On the Taneytown road...Gen [William] Barksdale is buried and near him Captain Foster *[sic]* from near Farm School in Centre County. I recollect well of meeting him in our tent after the battle of Fredericksburg."

With such a clearly marked grave site, the captain must have been transported to his home for permanent burial, for he is not now known to inhabit one of the small honored parcels in the National Cemetery at Gettysburg.

Captain Joseph A. Hubbard,
Company B, 2nd New Hampshire Infantry,
3rd Brigade, 2nd Division, 3rd Corps

Captain Joseph A. Hubbard,
2nd New Hampshire Infantry.

Joseph Hubbard had entered the service from Manchester, New Hampshire as second lieutenant of Company I. He was twenty-eight years old when killed on July 2. His death was described as occurring near the John Wentz house which stood within the confines of Sherfy's peach orchard along the Emmitsburg Road. When the 2nd New Hampshire made its last stand at this place, the captain was struck down. A member of the regiment related this scene:

Here, also, Captain Hubbard,...received his death wound. He was shot in the forehead, but regained his feet and wandered aimlessly about for some time after the rebel column had passed him. Some of his company who were captured learned from their rebel guards that he lived about two hours. Being a Mason, and having an emblem displayed, his body was buried and his grave carefully marked by members of the order in the rebel ranks, so that the body was subsequently recovered and identified.

The burial of Hubbard by the Masonic brotherhood is one of the most common threads one notices, which weaves continuously through the historiography of the Civil War. In fact, a Southern officer from Georgia was interred with great care by Masons of the *Union* Army just one-quarter mile north of where Captain Hubbard had been tenderly laid to rest.

Private Samuel Spear, Company B, 42nd Pennsylvania Infantry, 1st Brigade, 3rd Division, 5th Corps

Late on July the second, the Pennsylvania Reserves made an attack through Plum Run Valley just west of Little Round Top to clear out Confederates who were then in the southeastern portion of Mr. Rose's ruined wheatfield. A member of the "Bucktails" portrayed the unforgettable and horrible death of a young soldier. As the disorganized companies of the 42nd approached a stone wall on what is now called Houck's Ridge, two artillery projectiles were fired into their ranks by either a "Confederate gun from an exposed knoll" or from a Union battery nearby. The "Bucktail," William Rauch, explained:

...a shell from the rear passed over the heads of Company C. One of the men said, "Captain, that means us." The Captain [N.B. Kinsey] replied, "No, that is one of our own shells, and is meant for those fellows in the rocks." A moment later another shell came, taking off the arm of a Company B boy. The boy sprang up, crying, "I won't die, I won't die." Then for a moment, he ran in a circle, the blood spurting from the stump, before he dropped dead. The same shell also killed a man from Company I, hit the wall throwing part of it up in the air, and wounded seven or eight men." [including Captain Kinsey]

This scene must have remained with Rauch until he died. My research determined that the "Company B" boy had to be Spear, as he was the only man of that company killed on July 2. The whereabouts of Spear's body have not been determined. His hometown was Duncannon, Pennsylvania.

Second Lieutenant Isaac A. Dunsten, Company C, 105th Pennsylvania Infantry, 1st Brigade, 1st Division, 3rd Corps

When I first read this account of the army officer, so vividly remembered by Mrs. Anna M. Holstein, I wanted especially to include it in my book.

However, his name was not mentioned specifically. I finally ascertained it as accurately as possible, by researching every Pennsylvania lieutenant mortally wounded at Gettysburg, and particularly any who died in the hospital wards administered by Mrs. Holstein at Camp Letterman. Lieutenant Dunsten, twenty-three and single, who died on August 26, fit all of the criteria. Here is Nurse Holstein's recollection.

> In the officers' row lay, for some weeks, a young lieutenant, from Schuylkill County, Penn., with both thighs shattered, suffering fearfully. A few hours before his death, at his request the Holy Communion was administered to him; after joining in the solemn services, he remained perfectly still—unconsciously "passing away," as those present thought,—until a glee club, from Gettysburg, going through the hospital, singing as they walked, paused at his tent and sung—without knowing anything of what was passing within—"Rally round the Flag." The words and the music seemed to call back the spirit to earth, and forgetting his crushed limbs and intense suffering, sprang up, exclaiming: "Yes, boys, we did 'rally round the flag;' and you will rally oft again!" then sank back exhausted, and soon was at rest.

Lieutenant Dunsten was buried the following day in the graveyard of the hospital which sat on a ridge south of the main grounds. Dunsten was one of twenty-three casualties the "Wild Cat" regiment bore on July 2 while fighting along the Emmitsburg Road a hundred yards or so north of the peach orchard.

 ### Private Erastus A. Allen,
Company I, 145th Pennsylvania Infantry,
4th Brigade, 1st Division, 2nd Corps

One of the few military chaplains still actually a member of a fighting regiment at this period of the war, was Reverend John Stuckenberg, from Erie, Pennsylvania, mentioned earlier, who had enlisted in the 145th in 1862. On July 3 he visited what was then the first encampment of the Second Corps hospital, located on the west bank of Rock Creek on the Bushman and Schwartz farms. In his diary Stuckenberg mentioned Private Allen, saying:

> [I] went back to the hospital, where I found quite a number of our wounded....I found the surgeons & nurses busily engaged with the wounded, scattered around in all directions, some lying on blankets, some on straw, a few on stretchers, others on the bare ground. E. Allen of Co. I, shot through the abdomine [sic] suffered terribly. Some of the intestines protruded through the wound & some of their contents would occasionally flow out, producing a horrible stench.

On the 4th of July during a very heavy rain, Stuckenberg worked for hours to cover the wounded since, as he said, "there was not a hospital tent at our hospital." After the rain, he procured some hay and placed this under some of the injured men. He also tore up a few old blankets and ponchos to cover the soldiers, reporting that, "I gave my rubber blanket to one of our men, my woolen one to Wm. Brown, & tour [sic] another woolen one belonging to Lt. Col. [David B.] McCreary & divided it between E. Allen & H. of Co. I.''

The next day, Sunday, July 5, the 145th left the battlefield; but before the chaplain joined them he noted: "I was sick on the morning of the 5th and concluded to go somewhere in the country to rest & recruit. I first buried E. Allen who had died at 8 the evening previous, took the names of all our wounded & did all I could for them.''

Allen had been mortally wounded on July 2 in or near the notorious wheatfield on the George Rose farm, where about eighty of his comrades were also struck down. His initial grave site was on the Jacob Schwartz farm near a place referred to as "Red Rock." He was later removed to the National Cemetery where his body remains today.

Private John Edmonds, Battery H, 1st Ohio Light Artillery, 3rd Volunteer Brigade, Artillery Reserve

Sometime late on the afternoon of July 2, Private Edmonds received a gunshot wound which resulted in a compound fracture of the left ankle. His battery was then positioned in a cornfield on Cemetery Hill. Edmonds was eventually taken to the Eleventh Corps hospital which was bivouacked on the George Spangler farm near the "Granite Schoolhouse" just south of Powers' Hill. His leg was first amputated about the "middle third." While at this hospital he came under the care of Justus M. Silliman, 17th Connecticut Infantry, who nursed him until his death.

Private Silliman, writing home to his mother at ten o'clock on the evening of July 15, remarked:

> Have been very busy this afternoon attending to the wounded. One poor fellow who occupied this tent has left this world of suffering and gone to Jesus in whom he trusted. he was a fine intelligent man, was superintendent of the sabbath school in the town at which he enlisted, his name is John Edmonds, Co. H, 1st Ohio light artillery. he leaves a mother and sisters to whom he a short time previous had dictated a letter. he had his leg amputated twice.

Twenty-three-year-old Edmonds was soon interred at the Spangler farm's new military cemetery and was then removed a few weeks afterward to the National Cemetery a mile away for permanent burial. He was one of only two deaths in that battery, and his grave is barely fifty yards away from the location Battery H occupied during the battle, and where Private Edmonds received his death wound.

Second Lieutenant Amaziah J. Barber, Company H, 11th United States Infantry, 2nd Brigade, 2nd Division, 5th Corps

It is the natural inclination of a wounded man left on a battlefield or in a field hospital to do anything in his power to get word of his condition to his family. A few of these poignant letters and telegrams still exist, but they are quite rare. The following correspondence illustrates this painful situation most acutely.

Hospital 2d Div 5th Corps
near Gettysburg

A. Barber
Burlington Iowa

I have lost my left leg above the
knee. Will be here three weeks.

A.J. Barber
2d Lt. 11th Infantry

What a terrible and frightening bit of news this must have been for Barber's family in Iowa. Still, there appeared to be hope. The lieutenant gave no reason not to believe he would make it. He had written the above less than two weeks after the battle, when the events of his wounding, which took place somewhere just west of Little Round Top possibly along John Houck's ridge, were still clear in his mind. However, Lieutenant Barber chose to leave out all but the essentials.

Attached to Barber's note was this communication:

Gettysburg July 14, 1863

Mr. A. Barber
Dear Sir
I was this day requested by Lieut. Barber to forward the above by telegraph but finding that impossible I take the next best course & sent it by mail. Lieut. B. is lying at the Hospital above named, about 5 miles south of this place, where I have been engaged in tending the wounded for several days. He seemed to me to be doing very well, & yet his case is doubtless attended with some hazard. He was amputated above the knee & has no other wounds. Is faithfully taken care of.

Truly yours
George R. Bliss
Prof's in the University
at Lewisburg, Pa.

"His case is doubtless attended with some hazard." These few words said it all. The situation was not so satisfactory after all. That short sentence must have sent a cold chill and tightened the heart of any loved one who read it. But almost another two weeks passed before Lieutenant Barber died; the day was the 26th of July, 1863.

In a report written on July 16 from Berlin, Maryland by the commander of the 11th Infantry, Major De L. Floyd-Jones, Barber was noted to be still surviving, with *both* legs amputated above the knee.

Amaziah Barber was originally from New York and had enlisted as a private on January 8, 1862. By February 1863 he had risen through the ranks to corporal, sergeant, first sergeant, sergeant major and then second lieutenant. His service was generally with Company H, where he was brevetted First Lieutenant on July 2 for "gallant and meritorious service at the battle of Gettysburg, Pa...."

For some unknown reason, Barber's body was not buried in the National Cemetery but in Evergreen Cemetery, the private burial ground contiguous to it, and which is well known for its important position within the Union lines during the battle. A few other Gettysburg casualties were interred there also.

Second Lieutenant Silas A. Miller, Company A, 12th United States Infantry, 1st Brigade, 2nd Division, 5th Corps

The 12th regiment of "Regulars" consisted of only eight line companies and was raised in New York City and Albany, New York; Essex, New Jersey and counties in both Indiana and Iowa. At Gettysburg their losses were 92 out of 453 present. One of those was Lieutenant Miller who had enlisted in August 1861 in New York as a private in Company A. One letter survives which chronicles his final minutes on July 2. As it is perpetually good fortune to locate such a document, the dispatch is quoted in full, just as it was written.

Camp nr Wheatfield, Va.
July 18th 1863.

Mr. C.W. Miller
    Dr Sir,
    In answer to your's of the 11th inst: just received, it is my painful duty to inform you that the report is perfectly true, that your brother was killed by a musket ball on July 2nd near Gettysburg, Pa: His body was recovered from the field and buried the same night.
    I wrote you on July 3rd, directing the letter to the Metropn Bank giving the circumstance of his death and burial. Have you ever received the letter? We had great difficulty in mailing letters, and it may have miscarried.
    The Regt: went into action about 5. P.M. July 2, and was under a very severe fire for some time from the enemys sharpshooters. I think your brother must have been hit, about 6. P.M. He was shot through the body, near the heart.—said, Oh! God, I am shot.—was moved to a rock near, and only lived about ten minutes, he spoke no more, was unable, & evidently expected death, he seemed free from pain, nothing could be done for him of any avail. He died on the field, gallantly doing his duty.
    He was a great favorite in his Regt: and is much regretted. His brother officers desired me to convey to his family, the sincere condolence of the

73

The grave of Lieutenant Silas A. Miller was temporarily located in the general area as shown in the foreground of this modern photograph. The site of John Rose's wheatfield, in and around where so many men were killed, is situated in the background.

Regt. in the loss they have sustained.

His valise, sword, belt, sash, ring pocket-book & some letters were saved, and will be sent to where you may wish, on the first opportunity.

He was buried at 10 P.M. on July 2nd in the enclosure of the nearest Log House to the field, on the side road near Sugar Loaf Hill [or Little Round Top, as it is now called], at Gettysburg, seventeen paces southwest of house, on side of stone fence nr. Pear tree. A board was put up at the head of the grave, marked with name &c and a small book with his name written on several pages, buried on his person.

Capt [Thomas S.] Dunn desires me to acknowledge the receipt of a letter from your Father, this letter will answer both; our stationery &c is very limited.

Again tendering my sincere condolence & best wishes for your family—

I am
Dr Sir
Very truly Yrs.
(Sd.) B.P. Mimmack.
Lt. & Adjt. 12th Infy.

The lieutenant was fortuitous to have had such a distinctly marked grave site. The log house mentioned is probably that of John Weikert, the grounds of which were used as an ambulance collecting point on the second of July. Today his remains are honorably buried in the U.S. Regulars section of the National Cemetery nearby.

 ### Private William Walton,
Company E, 155th Pennsylvania Infantry,
3rd Brigade, 2nd Division, 5th Corps

The 155th lost six killed during the Battle of Gettysburg when they engaged a portion of General Jerome Robertson's Texas and Arkansas brigade late on July 2 along the west slope of Little Round Top. The historian of the regiment explained many years later what happened to Private Walton, an occurrence quite common on Civil War battlefields.

> Private William Welton *[sic]*, of Company E, who was instantly killed in the Confederate's attack on Little Round Top, on the afternoon of July 2d, was shot in the throat....

As showing how little incidents produce unexpected results, in the case of William Welton, his messmates, Privates Chas. F. McKenna and James P. O'Neil, immediately after this, his fatal wound, took the contents of his pockets from his body, consisting of a prayer book and some letters to his affianced, with a view of sending the articles to his family. This action occurred in the middle of the battle, the comrades named not being allowed to leave the ranks long enough to take the body of their messmate to the rear. The stretcher-bearers appeared and helped to place the body on the stretcher, and it was carried away to the rear. The messmates named, being obliged to resume loading and firing in the ranks, knew not to what point the body was carried by the stretcher-bearers. This friendly action of Welton's messmates resulted in the loss at his burial in the rear of all data to indicate his name, rank or regiment, so that Private Welton was buried in a grave marked "name unknown."

Private William Walton,
155th Pennsylvania Infantry.

Private Walton's burial site has still not been identified, and if ever found was more than likely consigned to one of the numerous "Unknowns" which now dot the historic landscape of the National Cemetery at Gettysburg.

Corporal Samuel M. Caldwell, Company D, 118th Pennsylvania Infantry, 1st Brigade, 1st Division, 5th Corps

Although the Fifth Corps of the Army of the Potomac was heavily engaged during the late afternoon of July 2 along the Millerstown crossover road, near and in the wheatfield, and through Plum Run valley, the 118th, which was part of that corps, fortunately lost only three men killed or mortally wounded that singularly bloody day. The fate of one of those soldiers, as related by a member of one of the New Jersey regiments in the Third Division, Sixth Corps, is here told. It remains one of the most memorable I have ever encountered.

Between perhaps 11:30 p.m. and midnight of July 4 a small burial party aided by the light of a low, pale moon and the stub of a small candle moved cautiously over the late battlefield near the Millerstown road and a little north of Rose's now badly trampled and sullied wheatfield. Here they found

> ...one body, that of a young, light-haired boy, not over nineteen at the furthest, whose forehead was pierced by a ball; in his left hand he firmly grasped his rammer; his right hand or its forefinger was in the watch-pocket of his pantaloons. We examined this pocket and found in it a small silver shield with his name, company, and regiment engraved upon it. We took possession of this momento, and fortunately finding a fragment of a cracker-box, marked upon it in pencil, by moonlight, the inscription found on the shield. We buried him with two of his comrades, one of whom belonged to the Fifth Corps, and placed the rude board at the head of his grave in the hope that it would some day enable some pilgrim-friend to find the body. Since that day the shield has been sent to the soldier's father; its inscription was, "S.L. Caldwell, Company D, 118th Pennsylvania Volunteers."

An actual witness to Caldwell's death stated that he was killed when the 21st Mississippi advanced upon the right flank of the 118th and was "so near, in fact, that Corporal S.M. Caldwell, Company E, was shot through the right side of the head at close quarters...."

It is notable that although Caldwell is now interred in the National Cemetery at Gettysburg in D-6 of the Pennsylvania Plot, the state's military records show him as having been killed at Shepherdstown, [West] Virginia on September 20, 1862 just a few days after the Battle of Antietam.

The foregoing illustrates well the aid in which "identification discs" or "dogtags" can be used to properly secure the final disposition of a soldier's corpse. Unfortunately, "ID" tags were not issued during the American Civil War, but some were purchased privately through sutlers or jewelers. This is the only case that I have ever read of its actual use to identify a body.

 ### Private Charles F. Howard,
Company I, 2nd New Hampshire Infantry,
3rd Brigade, 2nd Division, 3rd Corps

A strange incident is connected to this man's death, as you shall see in a moment. Charles Howard was wounded on July 2 in or near the peach orchard or along the Emmitsburg Road. He was captured and became one of the few Federal soldiers led to the John Cunningham farm along Marsh

Creek which was taken as a field hospital for Wofford's Brigade, of McLaws' Division, Longstreet's Corps. A daughter of Mr. Cunningham remembered Howard, who was then twenty-one, and had been born at Grantham, New Hampshire. However, in the years prior to the Civil War he was living in Plainfield. She wrote this a generation later:

> Until after the surrender, no letters could be gotten through the Confederate lines, but father notified the families of all the Union wounded who were brought to his place. Among many others, the sister of one badly wounded man, Ellen Howard of Meriden, New Hampshire, started at once for Gettysburg. And on the train a stranger engaged her in conversation, asking if, should she find her brother dead, she had money enough to bring the body home. She had not, and he opened his purse and handed her forty dollars. The brother had died [on July 18] before she arrived.

This is just one more curious incident in the neverending battlefield lore of Gettysburg.

Private Martin J. Coleman,
5th Massachusetts Light Artillery,
1st Volunteer Brigade, Artillery Reserve

The story of the death of this eighteen-year-old Boston artilleryman began on July 2 in the late afternoon as the 5th Massachusetts Battery engaged Confederates attacking the "peach orchard" line just southwest of the Abraham Trostle farm buildings. Coleman was tragically wounded when he was struck by a bullet and suffered a compound fracture of the right humerus. In the evening retreat the battery left Coleman behind, and his comrades were unsure of his fate until two days later. The following diary entries of Corporal Thomas E. Chase give us part of the picture.

> July 3, 1863. Martin J. Coleman and Henry W. Soule still missing....
> July 4, 1863. Martin J. Coleman found on the field seriously wounded, a.m. He was brought to the rear and carried to the hospital....

What had happened to help locate Coleman was the order of Captain Charles A. Phillips to Corporal Benjamin Graham to go beyond the pickets to secure a pole-yoke from a disabled limber left on the field between the two armies. Graham detailed his adventure:

> So I went out on the centre of the field, and tried to get it, but as I had no wrench, and there was none in the limber chest, I had to leave it. I walked from there in the centre of both picket lines, to the position we occupied on the second day. It was there where I found poor Henry Soule. He was the first one that I found. He was under a small apple tree. [Edward] Fotheringham was nearer the position of the Battery.
> From the field I went into the Trostle house, where I found John Hathaway and Coleman. They were both badly wounded. The rebels had stripped Hathaway of all his clothing. When I found him he was sitting in a chair underneath a mirror, and I saw him in the glass first, and he gave me quite

a fright, for the only thing he had on was a white sheet. He looked more like a ghost than a man. I asked him if there were any other of the boys in the house, and he said he did not know, so I looked the house over from garret to cellar, and there, behind the chimney, found Coleman. I tried to get an ambulance to take them to the rear, but it was of no use. I went back to the Battery and reported to the Captain. He had the men make some stretchers, and had Hathaway and Coleman taken to the field hospital, where they died in a day or two. The last I saw of Henry Soule they were digging a grave under that apple tree, but I did not stay to see whether he was buried there or not.

Corporal Chase's diary imparted once again:

July 5, 1863. Sunday. Went to the hospital this morning and had my wound dressed. No hopes of the recovery of Martin J. Coleman....

July 6, 1863. By request of M.J. Coleman wrote to his father that he could not live, and that the letter would probably be the last he would hear from him. The Dr. has no hopes of Coleman's recovery....

In 1899 Thomas Chase stated that "writing that letter was the most pathetic act I was called upon to perform while in service. He dictated this to me: —'Dear Father: I have not long to live. I have tried to be a faithful soldier, and I die for the flag.'"

Martin Coleman expired on July 16 at the Artillery Reserve hospital located three miles from Gettysburg on the Baltimore Pike in a "good dwelling house and a barn." His burial place is not known to me at this time.

 **Second Lieutenant William J. Cockburn,
Company H, 120th New York Infantry,
2nd Brigade, 2nd Division, 3rd Corps**

An officer of the 80th New York Infantry gave a touching account of the suffering of this twenty-nine-year-old man from Kingston, who had been wounded in the thigh on the late afternoon of July 2. This was about the time a portion of Longstreet's Confederate division struck part of General Daniel Sickles' line near the peach orchard area along the Emmitsburg Road, causing them to fall back nearly one half mile.

The night [July 2] was very dark, but the low moans of the wounded, as they broke upon the chilly air, guided us in our search....One, among those wounded men—an officer of the 120th N.Y. Vol.—I had known long and well. He had grown up, surrounded by every luxury a refined and cultivated mind could demand and affluence could supply. His generous impulses— his social qualities—his ready wit—his bright intelligence— had made him an universal favorite. He had but recently exchanged the cheverons on his sleeve for the Lieutenant's strap, and in the retreat of the Third corps, was one among the hundreds left upon the field, wounded beyond recovery.

I can never forget his calm demeanor as he lay upon the damp earth, patiently waiting his turn to be cared for. While his young life was ebbing away, he was as composed as he could have been sitting by his mother's fireside.

He was anxious only to give us no trouble, and shut up his anguish in his own breast. No external exhibition of suffering could have touched me as did his unmurmuring submission to the fate that had befallen him.

While I could imagine what he suffered—from his wound less than from the consciousness that all his life-hopes and promises were thus cruelly blighted—I could not but envy the calm resignation of Lieutenant Cockburn.

The lieutenant did not immediately die of his wound. He was transported to a hospital thirty-five miles northward at Harrisburg, Pennsylvania where he succumbed to a secondary hemorrhage on July 22, 1863. No pen could have possibly painted a more worthy portrait of Lieutenant Cockburn than we have just read. He truly must have been one of the best that this country has ever produced. I would give much to have known him.

Private Jonathan E. Leavitt, Company D, 12th New Hampshire Infantry, 1st Brigade, 2nd Division, 3rd Corps

This twenty-four-year-old enlisted man had been born in Danbury in 1839. Wounded late on July 2 during the fighting east of the Emmitsburg Road, and just north of the Joseph Sherfy house, a friend finally found him, although it was too late to save his life. Here is the story as narrated by Richard Drake.

On Saturday morning, following the fight of Thursday afternoon, a soldier of another regiment called and inquired for me. He said that a comrade of mine, badly wounded, was at the 6th Corps hospital and wanted to see me. I at once hastened to the place indicated and there on a stretcher I found Jonathan Leavitt, of Sanbornton, a tent mate, in a terrible condition. Both feet and ankles had been crushed by a cannon ball or shell. By mistake he had been carried to the 6th Corps hospital, the stretcher placed under an apple tree and there he had lain for 40 hours unattended. His feet had turned black and were fast becoming a mass of corruption. Scores of surgeons not far off were operating on men of the 6th Corps, but this poor man, desperately wounded as he was, had received no attention whatever. Perhaps it was because the diamond on his cap indicated that he belonged to the 3d Corps and there were men of their own corps just as much in need of assistance as was he. I say this may have been the case, so I will make no reflections. My first act was to give my comrade a drink of water and then I attempted to find some surgeon who would dress his wounds, but all were too busy even to hear my story. I then hastened back to camp and called on Hiram W. Ferrin, Uriah H. Kidder, and Orren G. Colby to assist me, and together we carried Comrade Leavitt two miles to the 3d Corps hospital, where we found Dr. H.B. Fowler, who gave him immediate attention. Dr. Fowler administered ether at once and then placed the poor fellow on the amputation table, but before removing him from the stretcher he passed his knife through the mass of flesh and bones and left his feet and ankles on the stretcher. Dr. Fowler amputated both stumps and such was the demand for help that my offer to assist was gladly accepted. The poor fellow died in the operation.

Young Leavitt was evidently aware of his critical condition, but anxious to live. On the road to the hospital we met a regiment of cavalry, and the surgeon stopped and looked at Leavitt's wounds. "Well, doctor," said Leavitt, "is there any chance for me?" "Yes, there may be," replied the surgeon slowly. The last words the poor fellow spoke, addressed to Dr. Fowler, were of the same tenor, "Shall I pull through, doctor?" "Oh, yes, you are young and I hope so," was the reply.

Drake mentions that the Third Corps badge on Leavitt's cap may have prevented his receiving prompt medical aid. During my research for a book on the wounded at Gettysburg, I did find two other sources which demonstrated that this was not an uncommon practice by some medical officers in the Army of the Potomac.

Private Augustus Koenig,
Company B, 1st Minnesota Infantry,
1st Brigade, 2nd Division, 2nd Corps

During an early evening July 2 attack into Nicholas Codori's "thicket," when the 1st Minnesota suffered over seventy percent casualties, Private Koenig, thirty-one, and who had been wounded previously at Bull Run, Virginia, was shot. He died later that night or the next day at a field hospital on the farm of Nathaniel Lightner, which sat below Powers Hill along the Baltimore Turnpike, a couple of miles south of Gettysburg. A member of the regiment conveyed the sad fortunes of Augustus Koenig many years afterwards.

During the artillery bombardment prior to three o'clock p.m. on July 3, Private Charles Muller said:

> I do not know how many pieces were in action, but I think that we must [have] had about 3 or 4 hundred reports every minute and sometimes it was just a continual roaring. There was a man of our regiment lying up in the corner of the fence dead and some men went there to bury him and after they got through and left and were gone about 15 yards a cannon ball struck the grave and strew the ground all round. His name was Konick [sic] but he was mostly known by the name of Beerkeg because he was a brewer by trade and was about as thick as long, but he was a very good soldier....
>
> In 1897 when we were down at Gettysburg I asked Mr. Lightner (that was the name of the farmer that owned the ground) if [he] did find some of the balls that were fired [on that day] and he said they were so thick that a man could not walk over it without stumbling on some....and Mr. Lightner told me that all the dead that were buried on his farm are still resting on the grounds and that none of them were ever took up.

This poses an interesting question. Are Private Koenig and others still interred on that old farm? There is no doubt that a number of Northern soldiers and many Confederate bodies were never recovered nor accounted for. If so, Private Koenig deserves a better fate.

Private Hushai C. Thomas, Company D, 19th Maine Infantry, 1st Brigade, 2nd Division, 11th Corps

In a letter to her brother written on July 29, 1863, volunteer nurse Emily Souder detailed the burial of this private soldier, a single man from Morrill, Maine, who had been wounded about dusk on July 2 along Cemetery Ridge. The place where this incident happened was the first camp of the Second Corps hospital along Rock Creek.

A young man of the 19th Maine died last Tuesday. Everything that day was hurry and bustle, as the encampment was being removed to a new spot at some distance from the former one. I prevailed, however, on the nurse, with the authority of the ward-master, to put a clean shirt and drawers on him, and they promised to let me know when he was buried. When called, Mrs. Curtis, Mrs. Campion and Miss Raymond went with me to the spot where the body of this Maine boy lay, in a wide, shallow grave, beside a Pennsylvanian, each wrapped in his blanket, and the name of each written on paper pinned on his breast. I returned to camp, the men detailed for this duty agreeing to wait, and found the Rev. Mr. Parvin, who performed the burial service. Very often through the day we see dead men carried out. Indeed, I have learned to know whether the person carried on the stretcher is dead or living, by noticing whether he is carried with his head or his feet toward the shoulders of his bearers.

Thomas was subsequently moved, as were over 3,500 others, to the new Soldiers' National Cemetery which was dedicated that fall on November 19, 1863.

Corporal William C. Schultz, Company I, 71st Pennsylvania Infantry, 2nd Brigade, 2nd Division, 2nd Corps

Schultz, a twenty-one-year-old, single Philadelphian was wounded in both thighs in the late evening of July 2 along Cemetery Ridge, and died on the 29th of September at Camp Letterman hospital. He was interred for a time at the hospital cemetery and thereafter was moved to the National Cemetery, as is recollected here by a nurse, Mrs. Anna Holstein:

....Another, the only child of a widowed mother, (Mrs. Shultz [sic] of Norristown, Penna) lay from July until October, calmly bearing untold agony from a wound which he certainly knew must result in death; yet his one anxious thought, constantly expressed, was: "Mother, do not grieve; it is best, and right; bury me with my comrades on the field." So, at sunrise one bright autumn morning, his soul went up to God, —the casket which had held it, we laid to rest among the nation's honored dead in Gettysburg Cemetery.

This bereaved mother, who gave her all for her country, —her eldest upon Antietam's hard-fought field, Willie at Gettysburg, —with the thousands of others who have made the same precious offering, are names to be gratefully remembered and cherished while the record of this war endures.

Private Patrick J. Lannegan,
Battery A, 1st Rhode Island Light Artillery,
Artillery Brigade, 2nd Corps

The cruel death and subsequent burial of Private Lannegan, who was lead driver of No. 6 gun, were witnessed by a member of Battery A, Thomas Aldrich. Lannegan's "mortal" wound came about as the battery was firing into a Georgia brigade which had reached the Union line on Cemetery Ridge around sunset of July 2. Aldrich divulged the facts as follows:

> It is a singular coincidence that every man in the battery who was killed was a driver. Two of them were working the guns when killed. Lannegan, my lead driver, was holding his horse when shot. As our battery was being relieved at that time and just as the enemy were retreating down the hill, Lannegan begged me to take him from the field. Lieutenant [Jacob] Lamb put a man in charge of my horses, and I took Lannegan on my back and carried him to the hospital, remaining with him until I had placed him on the operating table. When it was found that his stomach refused whisky the surgeons would not operate upon him, and he was laid out to die. I entreated the surgeons to give him proper treatment, but it was of no avail. The Sisters of Mercy, who were at the hospital, took charge of him....Lieutenant [Alonzo] Cushing was buried that morning [July 3] not far from our camp, also...Lannegan, near the hospital.

The official records of this battery show Private Lannegan, who was a resident of Providence, Rhode Island, to have been interred on the John Trostle farm north of Rock Creek, under a walnut tree. His body was later moved to the National Cemetery outside of Gettysburg. The burial place would suggest that the hospital of Battery A was somewhere between the Jacob Schwartz farm, which was the principal hospital of the Second Corps, and the Trostle farm, which was the main field hospital of the Sixth Army Corps.

Private Ernest Simpson,
Battery E, 1st Rhode Island Light Artillery,
Artillery Brigade, 3rd Corps

The United States army in the 1860s was not quite a "Foreign Legion" but there were a great many men in it who would have certainly fit the mold. One such soldier was Ernest Simpson, a man obviously not fighting for love of country, or to free black slaves. His type of soldier was by far not an uncommon portion of the Union Army at the time of Gettysburg. The regimental history of the battery sets forth the following:

> Corporal Simpson,...was more than an ordinary man, and had somewhat of a romantic history. Lieutenant [John K.] Bucklyn, in a communication to the Providence Sunday Star of June 11, 1882, says: "Ernest Simpson was my company clerk, and had begged permission to go into the battle. I told him we would probably be killed, and he must settle my accounts with the government. During the fight he came to me and asked permission

to take charge of a gun. I consented, and in a few minutes his head was shot off. He was a brave and noble soldier, who joined us at York, Pa., attracted by the great reputation of Rhode Island batteries. He had left home (Leipsic, Germany) because his parents opposed a love affair, attempted to commit suicide in London, and joined us with the expectation of being killed. He said I was his only friend in America, and he made a will in my favor, which I now have.

Private Simpson was buried on the south side of Joseph Sherfy's farm after the battle, then moved to the Rhode Island plot of the National Cemetery. The battery had been in action in the late afternoon of July 2 along the Emmitsburg Road in the environs of this man's aforementioned farm house.

Private James H. Riggin,
Battery F, 1st Pennsylvania Light Artillery,
3rd Volunteer Brigade, Artillery Reserve

During the early evening hours of July 2, Confederate troops under General Harry Hays and Colonel Isaac Avery boldly assaulted the Union line on east Cemetery Hill, and for a tense few minutes overran and held part of Batteries F and G Pennsylvania Artillery, commanded by R. Bruce Ricketts. At one stage of this partially hand-to-hand encounter in the dark, Ricketts stopped one of his men from clubbing to death a wounded Louisiana sergeant. Then, he noted:

> At about this time and near the same place James H. Riggin the guidon bearer staggered against me and fell with the cry "Help me, captain." When we found him after the fight he was dead and the sleeve of the right arm of my coat was covered with the brave fellows blood. We afterward learned that in a personal encounter with a Confederate officer who had attempted to capture the battery guidon, which was planted near the second gun from the left—he had shot the officer with his revolver, but at the same moment the staff of the guidon was shot in two and poor Riggin shot through the body.

The rear of the Evergreen Cemetery gatehouse showing the well near to where Privates J.H. McCleary and J.H. Riggin were buried.

83

Today the visitor may stand within just a few feet of where this bloody encounter took place—as it is easy to find the "second gun from the left" at the monument of Rickett's battery, which is only a short distance east of the Baltimore Pike across from the entrance to the National Cemetery.

The precise location of Private Riggins' grave came under question in 1864 which resulted in a conversation between David McConaughy of Gettysburg and Lieutenant C.B. Brockway of Battery F. In a letter dated March 27, 1864 Brockway replied to McConaughy's questions.

> You ask me "If James H. Riggin had any relatives and where they reside?" I believe he has a mother and sister living in Laurel, Sussex Co. Del. Immediately after the charge on Thursday evening, July 2nd, I had my men dig a grave in the Cemetery, and as it was dark did not pay much attention to its location. In that grave I placed the bodies of Seg't Myron French, and E.Y. Anderson of our Battery, and as a sort of protection placed above and below them palings from a neighboring fence. Riggin, who died in the night, was buried by their side next day, and the rest of our dead were scattered. In the name of my company I heartily thank you for noting the resting place of Riggin, and if we survive, in after years 'twill be a sad pleasure to visit his grave.

Mrs. Elizabeth Thorn caretaker of the Evergreen Cemetery lived in the brick gatehouse in 1863. After the battle she was instructed by Mr. McConaughy, president of the cemetery association, to commence burying corpses in that cemetery. Mrs. Thorn, whose husband was away in the army, along with her elderly father, buried 105 soldiers there, including a few Confederates. Fifteen of the 105 were interred near the well behind the gatehouse. All this was accomplished while she was about six months pregnant.

A portion of the Union Second Corps hospital on Jacob Schwartz's farm where several of the men noted died and were temporarily interred.

Part III
Friday, July 3, 1863

"Dead faces! How they haunt us! Lying all about the fields and beside every tree in the woods. Who are they? Whose father, or brother, or husband? Here is a body all broken and mangled. Who praised the symmetry of that form when last it stood in its native Northern village? Here is a face all black and swollen. Who was it that a few months ago called it beautiful?"

That last and fatal day opened furiously for many, even before the hazy sun broke above the green hills and soft meadows and dark woods around Gettysburg. Hours of mortal combat over Culp's and Bliss' and Spangler's farms, led out that day, and then it crested and finally dissolved upon the cultivated and rocky fields of farmers Frey and Small and Rummel and Lott. Seventeen thousand fell in that long ghastly twenty-four hours, and then the mighty armies turned away leaving their death and destruction behind. These are but a few who would remain forever to sleep at Gettysburg or along the rutted roads leading from that dreadful place.

Corporal James O. Butcher, Company D, 28th Pennsylvania Infantry, 1st Brigade, 2nd Division, 12th Corps

One of the musicians of the 28th Pennsylvania, whom we have heard of before, was William Simpson. He was detached during the battle to Surgeon H. Earnest Goodman who with other doctors had set up a field hospital at the farm of Abraham Spangler along the Baltimore Turnpike just south of Culp's Hill. On one occasion on July 3 while attending to his duties at this hospital Simpson

> saw quite a few of our boys at the hospital. One especially I will always remember. He was a corporal and had been badly wounded. They wanted

to amputate his leg. He said to me: "Will, they won't do it, for I will shoot the first man who touches me. I am married and I won't go home to be a burden on my wife." He was certainly earnest in every word he said. When the surgeons went over to him the second time intending to cut off his leg, he was dead.

After his death, which was probably much more of a burden to his beloved spouse, Butcher, a Philadelphian and the only corporal killed in the 28th, was buried on the north side of the Spangler farmhouse. Later he was taken up and reinterred in the Pennsylvania section of the Soldiers' National Cemetery at Gettysburg, barely one-half mile from where he died.

Sergeant William Timson Ambler, Company D, 57th New York Infantry. The oldest of four children of Thomas V. Ambler and Mary Ann Timson, he was born on September 9, 1844 in South Salem, New York. Sergeant Ambler died while fighting along Cemetery Ridge late on July 2. He was buried in the National Cemetery at Gettysburg.

Private Erastus B. Roberts,
Company B, 84th New York Infantry,
2nd Brigade, 1st Division, 1st Corps

The case of Private Roberts is another in which there may be some small doubt that he is the soldier actually described herein. but the evidence does point clearly in his direction.

On July 1, the 84th New York, heavily engaged near the Chambersburg Turnpike and near a "railroad cut or defile" northwest of Gettysburg, lost twenty-four men killed and mortally wounded. On July 3 this same regiment, also known as the "14th Brooklyn" or the "Brooklyn Chasseurs" or "Zouaves" was slightly engaged on the *right* of the Union line at Culp's Hill. Only one man was killed or mortally wounded here —E.B. Roberts, a thirty-seven-year-old soldier from Brooklyn. When the 84th moved to Culp's Hill it deployed near the 149th New York regiment who were holding the entrenchments at that place. A member of the 149th relived this horrible scene:

> Once when the regiment was out of the works and waiting in the hollow before described, a Brooklyn regiment in Zouave uniform was also waiting to be ordered to the front. It was whispered around that they were reputed to be a "Bully fighting regiment," and therefore attracted attention. They were mostly young men and presented a tidy and smart appearance. A musket ball struck a tree overhead and glanced downward into the breast of one of them as he reclined in the arms of a companion. He immediately gave a piercing scream which tore the hearts of thousands about him. It has been said that when a man is drowning the events of a lifetime pass quickly in review, but it seems impossible that a greater number of agonizing thoughts could be crowded into a short space of time than passed through the minds of many who heard that cry of despair. Visions of kind friends, a doting father, a loving mother, admiring sisters and affectionate brothers with hearts wrung with agony; yes, thoughts of a young life blighted, just as it had entered upon a period of usefulness and happiness, flitted through the mind as if on the wings of lightning. Ah! those who heard that piercing cry knew it was only the mortal expression of the terrible agony of a young heart as the cords were breaking which bound it to loved ones at home. His companions bore him tenderly away, and all were glad when they did so lest his condition made cowards of them all.

Who could ever forget such a scene? This description, read over one hundred years after the incident, still makes my blood run cold! Robert's military service records show that he was the only casualty of July 3. He was mortally wounded on that day and died on July 4, then buried in the Associate Reformed Graveyard in Gettysburg. In time, as many others were, Roberts was moved to the National Cemetery.

An 1864 view of the approximate spot where Lieutenant Jedediah Chapman Jr., 27th Connecticut Infantry was killed on July 2. It was said he "possessed a quick conscience, a clear mind, a ready hand, and was held in universal esteem." Round Top, on the southern end of the battlefield, can be seen in the distance.

Captain Thomas B. Fox,
Company K, 2nd Massachusetts Infantry,
3rd Brigade, 1st Division, 12th Corps

Many readers, especially those who are familiar with the entire Gettysburg battle, will recall the useless but destructive charge made by the 27th Indiana and 2nd Massachusetts on the morning of July 3, across Abraham Spangler's meadow just south-southeast of Culp's Hill. This attack was a disaster for the two regiments, the 2nd Massachusetts, alone, losing 134 men out of 316 engaged.

Captain Thomas Bayley Fox,
2nd Massachusetts Infantry.

Captain Fox was one of the fallen. A graduate of Harvard College, he was but eleven months in the service at this time, and already had passed through several hard campaigns and four major battles. In a little speech he made in August of 1862 at a recruiting meeting just prior to leaving for the front, Fox recited that, "the hour for mere enthusiasm [for the cause] had passed, and that the hour for obedience to principle and for action had come...." And as he closed the modest refrain he added: "Hereafter, if our lives are spared, should our children's children ask what we did for our country in this its great crisis, a blush such as never should be seen on an old man's face would come upon our faces if we were obliged to answer, — 'Nothing'."

An officer of Fox's regiment, Everett Pattison, said of him,

> Among the officers who bore honorable wounds on that day, was Capt. Tom Fox. He was one for whom I entertained a warm regard, and our friendship was mutual. Our ages were almost equal, both having been born in February, 1839. We graduated from college about the same time. When the war broke out we were both engaged in teaching, spending the hours not appropriated to school duties in studying law. Both of us had thrown our books aside to enter the service. He joined the regiment soon after I was

commissioned second lieutenant, and from that time our intimacy dated. I met him shortly after the action on the 3d, and he was then in the best of spirits. He was proud of his regiment and of what it had done on that day. A ball had struck him on the ankle, inflicting what all supposed to be a slight wound. "I will go home," he cheerfully said to me, "and get a little rest and visit my friends. This thing will soon heal, and I will be back by the time the regiment shall be called into action again." I bade him good-bye, without a thought that I had seen him for the last time. But the wound was more serious than we imagined, and in just three weeks afterwards he died.

The captain's father, writing after the war, placed Fox near the center of that seething meadow, endeavoring to rally his men when he was struck. Mr. Fox continued:

The wound was serious, but was not thought to be fatal. In a few days he was able to reach home, weak and weary....A sad change took place;...the previous strain upon the nervous system had been too great; fever, accompanied by delirium, supervened, and the fine constitution which he carried into the war, worn and shattered by the labors and exposures...refused to rally from the deep prostration. At four o'clock in the afternoon of July 25th he died, unconsciously and without a struggle, of sheer exhaustion.

At the burial of his body in Dorchester these lines were read: "....He fought for his country; who could leave a brighter record? He died for his country; who could wish a better epitaph?"

Private John Costello, Battery K, 5th United States Artillery, Artillery Brigade, 12th Corps

The 28th Pennsylvania drummer, Bill Simpson witnessed another death which was probably that of Private Costello. The time was approximately two o'clock p.m., July 3, when he explained:

The Artillery firing that preceded Pickett's Charge was terrific. The concussion was so great that the ground shook....It was horrible to see the men of the artillery dead and dying against their guns; their dead horses were all about them. I witnessed another terrible incident on Baltimore pike during the artillery engagement. Two pieces of Battery K, of the Fifth U.S. Artillery, had been placed on the right of the pike. The firing was so rapid that there was a premature explosion and the man at the sponge staff had both his arms blown off, and he was flung into a ditch. He was a splendid looking fellow before the accident, but a sight to behold afterward. I often wondered what became of him; in all probability he died.

John Costello was twenty-nine years old, born in King, Offaly County, Ireland and worked as a fireman before the war. He was the only man who was killed from the 5th "Regulars" during or after the battle. His records state that he was wounded in the chest by a shell and died on July 5 at the Twelfth Corps hospital (probably the George Bushman farm). The premature explosion of a shell would indeed wound a person in the chest area, especially if he lost both arms in the process.

The original wooden headboard carved for and placed over the grave of Second Lieutenant Manning Livingston, 3rd United States Artillery. This New York officer was killed in action on the David Klingle farm along the Emmitsburg Road late in the afternoon of July 2. The headboard is now on display as a memorial to Livingston at the Prince of Peace Episcopal Church in Gettysburg.

Private Gustavus Ritter,
Company D, 111th New York Infantry,
3rd Brigade, 3rd Division, 2nd Corps

There were ninety-five men killed outright or mortally wounded in this regiment during the battle, a very large number for any regiment to suffer, even one near to or at full strength.

Lieutenant Samuel B. McIntyre of Company A. remembered an incident which, although not written in great length or detail, followed the final moments of Private Ritter of Lyons, New York. McIntyre's regiment was located in a position along a stone wall which ran north to south through the now much dilapidated Brien farm on the crest of Cemetery Ridge. Around two o'clock p.m. on July 3, during the bombardment preceding Longstreet's assault, he remembered:

> Some three or four men thought there was some safety behind the barn, until a shell ripped through it tearing off a board and killed some of them, when they speedily returned to the regiment. A man of Co. D. whose name I now forget, had both his legs taken off below the knee. His comrades placed him just at our right, behind this barn, and he remained there until he died, holding up his poor bleeding stumps by his arms under his legs.

Ritter was thirty-three years old when he helplessly bled to death behind Abraham Brien's small wooden barn. His grave site has not been located as of this time, but his place of death is passed by thousands of people each year who travel the "auto tour" route at Gettysburg National Military Park. All drive within thirty feet of this exact spot.

Private Alfred G. Gardner, Battery B, 1st Rhode Island Light Artillery, Artillery Brigade, 2nd Corps

Anyone visiting the Rhode Island State House in Providence should not leave without paying their respects to the 12-pounder Napoleon smooth bore exhibited there. This piece, known as the "Gettysburg Gun," figured prominently in the fate of Alfred Gardner. Today that venerable old artillery tube and carriage, deeply scarred and heavily patinaed with age, stands silent, barely changed since the afternoon of July 3 when it last roared with fury, pointed out toward the rebel lines. The historian of the battery wrote that during the fierce cannonade preceding Pickett's and Pettigrew's advance,

one of the guns of Battery B was struck by a rebel shell, which exploded killing two cannoners who were in the act of loading. No. 1, William Jones, had stepped to his place in front, between the muzzle of the piece and wheel on the right side, and, having swabbed the gun, stood with sponge staff reversed (which is also the rammer) waiting for the charge to be inserted by No. 2. Alfred G. Gardner, No. 2, had stepped to his place, between the muzzle of the piece and wheel on the left side, and, taking the ammunition from No. 5, was in the act of inserting the charge when a shell struck the face of the muzzle, left side of the bore, and exploded. No. 1 was killed instantly by a fragment of the shell, which cut the top of the left side of his head completely off. He fell with his head toward the enemy, while the sponge staff was thrown two or three yards beyond him.

Alfred G. Gardner was struck in the left shoulder, almost tearing his arm off. He lived a few minutes, and died shouting: "Glory to God! I am happy! Hallelujah!" His sergeant and friend bent over him to receive his dying message; which was, to tell his wife that he died happy, and to send her his Bible.

Private Alfred G. Gardner,
1st Rhode Island Light Artillery.

91

Sergeant Albert Straight, commanding this gun, expressed that Gardner was known in the battery as "a pious man." Straight had been tenting with "old Mr. Gardner" as he was called, on the march into Pennsylvania. The twelve-pound cannon ball which Private Gardner was in the act of inserting into the muzzle when he was mortally wounded, is, as of this writing, still wedged solidly there, as it has been for over 128 years.

Alfred Gardner, from Middletown, Rhode Island, who was mustered into service August 12, 1862, may not have died immediately. His body was found buried on the grounds of a field hospital east of Michael Fiscel's farmhouse, a mile or so south of the battlefield. He was another whose remains were soon removed to the National Cemetery.

Sergeant William Henry Wikoff, Company H, 1st Minnesota Infantry. He was killed in the famous charge made by his regiment late on July 2 from Cemetery Ridge southwestward into Nicholas Codori's thicket. Wikoff, 28 years old when he died at Gettysburg, was buried in the cemetery in Easton, Pennsylvania. He was one of 79 Minnesotans who lost their lives as a result of the battle.

 ## Sergeant George O. Fell,
Company B, 143rd Pennsylvania Infantry,
2nd Brigade, 3rd Division, 1st Corps

At the time of the battle, J. Howard Wert was a teenager who lived south of Gettysburg on his father's farm near White Run. Writing in 1907 about the sacrifices of Union soldiers in the Civil War, he imparted:

George Ogden Fell was nothing to me. I never saw the young hero alive or dead. I never heard his name until I read his obituary in a religious journal of the day....[He] came from the little town of Waverly, Pennsylvania. He was a sergeant in company B, of the One Hundred and Forty-third Pennsylvania volunteers, one of the three regiments of Roy Stone's brave "Bucktail-Brigade" that left more than two-thirds of its entire membership dead or wounded on the slopes beyond the seminary.

Severely wounded in the hip, Young Fell was left upon the field within the enemy's lines. He was found two days afterwards in a private residence, placed there, probably, by the enemy, and was made as comfortable as circumstances would allow.

His father, who repaired immediately to the battlefield, had only the melancholy satisfaction of finding a mess of corruption, wrapped in a soldier's blanket, with a few inches of earth over it, but recognized it by marked articles of clothing as the body of his son. Unable to remove the body, and the National Cemetery being not yet planned, he secured for it decent burial in the grass-grown and ancient graveyard attached to the German Reformed Church, on High street, Gettysburg.

This was but one case of tens of thousands, at that same moment, darkening all the land and filling it with lamentations. Of a fine person and brilliant accomplishments, just ready to enter Yale College, with glittering prizes for honor and success opening before him and beckoning him onward, he dropped all, thrilled by his country's need, and at the age of eighteen, volunteered beneath the Stars and Stripes in the company in which his elder brother, who went unhurt through the fires of Gettysburg, was a lieutenant.[Asher M. Fell]

The name of George Ogden Fell today, like that of a million other heroes who fought and suffered, is but a misty memory.... What do we owe to George Ogden Fell and the 48,902 others of the Army of the Potomac who died in battle; to the tens of thousands of the same army who died of disease....?

In this interesting and moving article focused on granting pensions to Civil War veterans, Wert leaves the impression that Fell was wounded on July 1. This may have been true. Nonetheless, his military records testify that he was mortally wounded on July 3. This information could be correct even though the 143rd was but slightly engaged on that date when it assisted in the repulse of the so-called, "Pickett's Charge." In the days following the establishment of the Soldiers' National Cemetery, the body of Sergeant Fell was moved to the Pennsylvania section where it was noted and eulogized by Mr. Wert, and where his grave can be visited today.

Corporal Alfred G. Ryder,
Company H, 1st Michigan Cavalry,
2nd Brigade, 3rd Division, Cavalry Corps

The George Ryder family of Livonia, Michigan suffered the loss of two sons at Gettysburg. The ensuing letter was received by them several weeks after the battle.

July 8th, 1863
Gettysburg, Adams Co.
Pennsylvania -

Dear Mother;

I have desired a friend to say to you I have been in the last fight we have had; it was in and around Gettysburg near the Penna and Maryland line; I was wounded in the side by a ball. I am not without hope. The Lord willeth all things for good. I am in a hospital in Gettysburg, I hope you are all well and happy   from your affectionate Son

Alfred G. Ryder

Brother John is here also in one of the hospitals but not badly wounded.

Alfred was wrong about the fate of his brother, John, as shown by this next correspondence.

Gettysburgh *[sic]* July 9th/63

Mr. George Ryder.

Dear Sir:—Perhaps from other sources you have heard of your sons, both of whom are in the Service of their altar. John went with us in the 24th, and was killed on the 1st day of July near this place, and I buried him with my own hands. In my labors among the wounded at this place, in the various hospitals, I found Alfred—of the 1st Cavalry *[sic]* who was wounded, I believe on the 2d [3rd] and is now lying in a dangerous condition in a hospital, at the Union school House. I conversed with him for a long time. He does not expect to live. He is wounded through the left lung and it is with some difficulty that he breaths, *[sic]* and has lost the use of his limbs almost Entirely. I asked him if he had any word to send home. He gave me his testament to give to his mother. He has carried it with him through the war so far. He also said, Tell father to "do well by my brother, and when you look on him remember me."

William C. Way
Chaplain 24th Mich. Vols.

Private John Ryder, nineteen, of Company C, 24th Michigan, had been shot in the left portion of the chest. For a time afterwards it was believed by his mother that John had not been killed instantly. On September 15, 1863, a comrade, Alfred Noble wrote to Mrs. Ryder to reassure her that several soldiers believed that John had died instantly. The cavalryman who first wrote to her was John Passage, who suggested that John Ryder had not expired on the 1st but had lingered on for several days suffering until finally death released him from his pain. The truth may never be known, but Chaplain Way (as may have been his duty) conveyed in a letter July 12, that John had *not* suffered, and that he himself had marked the grave well so that "any one else can find it." In this same letter the chaplain sent word to the family that Alfred was "decidedly better," and that he "is not in so much danger from his wound as from an injury of his spine occasioned from a fall from his horse." The twenty-year-old Alfred appeared to be improving.

But, on July 18, in another communication to Mrs. Ryder, William Way explained: "Dear Madam. Your husband is here and in attendance upon Alfred who is very low, and from all appearances is sinking fast. I see that he grows weaker every day....Alfred seems to be so patient, so calm, so considerate, that my heart is all enlisted for him."

On July 20 Chaplain Way wrote in a letter to the Detroit *Advertiser* and *Tribune:*

William Williams and John L. Rider [John S. Rider, a different family altogether] of Co. B, 24th Michigan, died to-day. Alfred Rider [i.e. Ryder] of the 1st Michigan Cavalry will not probably survive through the night. His father is with him. He has given to his country two noble sons, Alfred, and John E., —the latter a member of the 24th, fell on the 1st July. Mr. Rider [sic] will soon return home with a sad heart....

Alfred stood it two more days and passed into eternity on July 22. The next day the good Chaplain Way, recounted the following to his hometown newspaper:

> Yesterday I buried Mr. Alfred Ryder, of the 1st Michigan Cavalry, and the body of his brother John E. Ryder, who fell July 1st, having been removed from the field and both rest together in the burying yard of the German Reformed Church.

Several months went by and then George Ryder contacted a local farmer about having the bodies of his two sons shipped home. Following is the uncorrected correspondence relating to that decidedly unpleasant task.

Gettysburg Nov 17th 1863

Mr. George Rider
Dear Sir

I took those bodies today and found the boxes by laying in the Ground so long all bursted so that I was compeled to have 2 new zinc Coffins made and also Rough boxes which just cost me coffins Boxes taken up and delivery at the depot $32.00 thirty-two Dollars, which would leave just $20.00 owing me which you will please send me by Express, for my trouble I make no bill only what it cost me. I should have sent the bodies to morrow morning but I had to get those Coffins made which will prevent me from sending before thursday morning So they will Start on the 19th from here. I have one Request to make and that is if you have the pictures Send me one of Each of them those small case photographs I have sent fourty to different parts and would like to have these pictures I have now already the most of them.

Yours Respectfully
John G. Frey

P.S. I was compeled to do what I did as the Express agts wouldt Express the bodies without it.

Gettysburg Dec 2d 1863

Mr. Rider
Dear Sir

I wrote to you some time ago or when I sent you the bodies of your sons that the boxes had been all bursted open and that they could not be sent without having zinc air tight coffins and Rough boxes out side my bill which I told you in my first letter was for the Rough boxes and taking up and delivery at the depot which was just what it cost me but when I had the bodies taken up I found that there would have to be new cases both out and inside which I got which makes the bill just twenty dollars more which if you have not sent yet you will please send soon as convenient as the person I had employed to furnish the coffins & Rough boxes is going to move to Ohio and wants his money and I will be oblige to advance it for him, which I will do. I hope you have Received the bodies in good order.

Yours Respectfully

John G. Frey

Gettysburg, Pa.

Is it not ironic that on the day that John and Alfred's remains were starting for Michigan, less than one mile away Abraham Lincoln was dedicating the Soldiers' National Cemetery to the memory of thousands of their comrades who would never leave this field of battle.

And another quite interesting note. Does it not seem unusual that the farmer J.G. Frey was collecting photographs of the dead men he had shipped all over the United States—forty so far? Frey was a man who took a strong interest in these matters. His private journal listing the burials of hundreds of soldiers in the Gettysburg area has been preserved to this day.

Captain George C. Thompson,
Company F, 69th Pennsylvania Infantry,
2nd Brigade, 2nd Division, 2nd Corps

This Philadelphia officer was another of those men who sometimes seem to sense their own mortality. One eyewitness remembered the scene.

> Numbers of the men seemed to have a premonition of death, and many stories are told of how they used to sit around the camp fire and predict the time. Captain Thompson as he sat by the camp fire at the foot of Benner's Hill *[sic]* the night of July 2 suddenly got up and said: "Well, boys, I shouldn't wonder if I leave you to-morrow, and when I do it will be quick." Next morning he mounted a caisson during the heat of the battle, and a shell bursting beneath him hurled him into eternity.

Thompson's records show that he was wounded in the head by a piece of shell and killed on July 3.

On July 10 an article in the Harrisburg, Pennsylvania *Daily Telegraph* noted this: "— buried near the left flank of the army where the charge was made were members of Company G, 69th Pa....—near the above, 'In memory of Captain George C. Thompson, Company F, 69th regiment Pennsylvania Volunteers.'"

This location was just in rear of an "angle" formed by a stone wall along Cemetery Ridge, and on the farm land of Peter Frey who lived on the Taneytown Road nearby.

Private James T. Bedell,
Company F, 7th Michigan Cavalry,
2nd Brigade, 3rd Division, Cavalry Corps

One of the most tragic deaths which occurred during the Gettysburg Campaign must have been that of cavalryman Bedell, who, frankly, was *murdered*. From the medical files of the Surgeon General's Office comes the testimony of Surgeon G.A. Otis:

> Private...Bedell...aged forty-two, was captured on July 3, 1863, at Gettysburg, his horse being shot from under him. He was hurried to the rear with other prisoners; in the subsequent retreat he was unable to keep up with the column, and all efforts to goad him on being unavailing, a confederate lieutenant, in command of the provost guard, cut him down, and left him for dead by the roadside. He was brought in by one of our scouting

The skull of Private James T. Bedell, 7th Michigan Cavalry, plainly shows the saber cut made by a Confederate officer who ruthlessly cut him down when he was unable to keep up with a column of prisoners being herded to the rear.

parties, and admitted to the Cavalry Corps Hospital. On July 25th, he was sufficiently rational to give the above account to Surgeon W.H. Rulison, 9th New York Cavalry. He was in a very depressed state at this time. His pulse was weak and beat from forty to forty-five per minute. He was indisposed to mental exertion; but when roused and interested, was quite rational. He lingered until August 15, 1863, the tendency to stupor becoming greater and greater towards the close. The autopsy revealed a sabre cut six inches long, which had raised an osseous flap, adherent at its base, from the left parietal, and a fracture of the right parietal, with great splintering of the vitreous plate. The sabre had penetrated the dura mater on the left side, and on the right side the meninges were injured by the depressed inner table. The posterior lobes of both hemispheres of the brain were extensively disorganized. The specimen with the above history was contributed by Surgeon W.H. Rulison, 9th New York Cavalry, since killed in battle.[near Winchester, Virginia, August 29, 1864]

This lamentable soldier from West Bloomfield, Michigan is another who is currently buried in the National Cemetery. His military service records indicate that he died at Camp Letterman General Hospital near Gettysburg on August 30, although Otis reports Bedell's death as August 15, 1863. The accompanying photograph aptly illustrates the brutality of humankind in war.

 ## Captain Ephraim Wood,
Company H, 125th New York Infantry,
3rd Brigade, 3rd Division, 2nd Corps

Just as the last of General James Pettigrew's exhausted Confederate infantry regiments were breaking up amidst the terrible musketry fire of Alexander Hays' division along Cemetery Ridge, Chaplain Ezra D. Simons of the 125th reminisced on what occurred next:

> When the rebel line broke, our color-sergeant, Harrison Clark, sprang over the wall and bore the flag proudly down the slope to the fence skirting the Emmettsburg *[sic]* road. In the shelling that preceded the charge, among others killed was John W. Defreest, a near relative of the writer; one who had passed with his brother and his captain, Ephraim Wood of H Company, through the rebel lines investing Harper's Ferry.
>
> Bravely standing behind that historic stone wall was the captain just named, who scorned the defence of even a low field-marking fence, and with needless boldness faced death. And death came. A bullet pierced his abdomen, and he was borne from the field to the hospital at Rock Creek, there—the next day—to die. Willard D. Green, of H Company, saw him the moment he was struck. Sergeant Jacob Houch and the writer kneeled at the brave dying man's side, who, after intense suffering, passed away, speaking with last breath the name of his wife. Captain Wood was always much interested in military affairs. He was, before the war, Captain of the Troy City Artillery Company. He was born May 14th, 1818. He was a man of true, firm principle. The writer once heard him, when he was asked to put his name to a paper, of the correctness of which he did not know, say:

"I cannot do it." When told, that he might venture to do it, he replied: "I will do right, though the heavens fall." His short career with the regiment, displayed, in all of its phases, from Harper's Ferry to Gettysburg, the qualities of a true man and a brave soldier. He died a true Christian.

Captain Ephraim Wood,
125th New York Infantry.

Captain Wood, then forty-five years old, was carried first to General George Meade's abandoned headquarters at the Lydia Leister farmhouse, where many of the wounded were collected to await ambulance transportation that would take them to the rear. Private Charles W. Belknap was one who helped to carry the captain to this place. Belknap remained with Wood until he was picked up. The next day, July 4, 1863, Private Belknap wrote in his diary that Captain Wood had died at six o'clock a.m. at the Third Division, Second Corps hospital.

Private Frederick Corcelins,
Company K, 5th Michigan Cavalry,
2nd Brigade, 3rd Division, Cavalry Corps

Two very interesting yet distressing letters endured which chronicle the destiny of this twenty-year-old cavalryman from near Ann Arbor, Michigan. Both are written by Frederick's brother, and you, the reader, may sense the hopefulness in one and then the dismay and frustration in the other.

Battle Field July 4th

Dear Mother,
 Our Army has gained a great victory. The battle has been raging with great fury for two days. There is a lull this morning. Our Division was engaged hand to hand with Stuarts cavalry. The Fifth were dismounted skirmishers. Fred was there and faced the music like a true soldier. I am pained but obliged to tell you that he is wounded and a prisoner in the hands of the enemy. I done everything in my power to rescue him. Went into the enemys lines late last night with a white flag for him. One of his company volunteered

to accompany me. He was with him when he was shot and bound up his wound and left him very comfortable. Do not worry for him. He is strong and brave as a lyon *[sic]*. The enemy took him to the rear to a farm house and promised me that he should have the very best of care. He will be parolled *[sic]* and left with a Union farmer and receive the best care in the world. The people here are so good and will do any thing for a Union soldier. I will try and get to him as soon as the enemy leave the ground. His partner who bound up his wounds thinks there is no bone broken. He is shot in the leg. I have his purse containing $40. I will either send it home or give it to him when I see him. Above all do not let this trouble you too much, for I am quite confident that it is not serious.

I believe he will recover and be all right again...such fighting I never saw before....

Edward

Upperville, Va July 21st

Dear Mother:

On the 4th I sent you a few hasty lines from the battlefield of Gettysburg conveying the sad enough intelligence that Fred had received a wound while fighting with his regiment on the right flank of our army. That news was bad enough but still with my usual hopefulness from the representations made to me of the nature of the wound I did not anticipate any very serious result to follow and sought to ease your mind with the assurance that in my opinion all would yet be well, not knowing that at the very moment those lines were being penned, the spirit of him to whom they referred had already taken its upward flight I trust to mingle eternally with the angels....As the chief engagement of the short [but] glorious campaign was drawing to a close...my brother fell pierced by a murderous bullet. Calm and heroic still he urged his companions to resume exertions if possible for the possession of a position which was of advantage to our side, and when it was apparent our boys were overpowered, the last cartridge being fired at the traitors, he ordered his faithful gun destroyed that it might not fall in their hands. They left him there...yet and just as the Fourth of July was to usher in memories that can never die, his spirit took its everlasting flight....

I will write again shortly.

Edward

The grave of Frederick Corcelins cannot be found in the Gettysburg area. His corpse then, was either shipped to Michigan or lies in an unmarked or "unknown" plot of ground somewhere in Adams County, Pennsylvania.

Corporal Adon G. Wills,
Company B, 72nd Pennsylvania, Infantry
2nd Brigade, 2nd Division, 2nd Corps

Mary W. Lee, a volunteer nurse, arrived in Gettysburg almost as soon as the battle smoke had cleared away. She worked for three months in the Federal Second Corps hospital and at Camp Letterman General Hospital.

A biographer of Mrs. Lee wrote in 1867:

> One of the patients who died here, on her hands, was Aaron [sic] Wills,
> color corporal in the Seventy-second Pennsylvania volunteers, the regiment
> in which her son was serving. A ball struck the flagstaff, and shattered it.
> Aaron wrapped the flag around his arm, and shouted, "Don't let the col-
> ors fall, boys!" The next moment a ball struck him in a vital part, and he
> fell, yet held the flag up so that it would not touch the ground, till it was
> taken from his faithful hands, and carried on at the head of the regiment.

A year after on the anniversary of his son's death, the father of Adon Wills
wrote an affecting letter to Mrs. Lee.

> To-day,...I walked out to the cemetery, to look at the little mound that covers
> the remains of my beloved boy. As I looked, the words of his last letter,
> those blessed words, came into my mind: "Father, do not worry at my be-
> ing in a dangerous position. I believe, as you say, I can die in no nobler
> cause; and, to tell you the truth, I would as soon die on the battle-field as
> I would a natural death." He need not have said, "to tell you the truth,"
> for he never told a lie.

Mary Lee ministered faithfully to many men in Ward B, 6th Division of
that hospital. Wills' military file, probably incorrectly, surmises that he perished on July 3 during the battle itself. In any event, let us place ourselves in
the melancholy mind of the father, as he stood yearly over the spot where
all of his worldly hopes and dreams lay rotting to dust. It is a place we do
not relish to linger for long.

Corporal Ira E. Sparry,
Company L, 1st Vermont Cavalry,
1st Brigade, 3rd Division, Cavalry Corps

Late on Friday July 3 plans were made to attack Confederate troops who
were in position facing the extreme left of the Union line just below Big Round
Top. There were two main reasons for this movement. One was, "to relieve
the Union left from the menace of these bodies of infantry entrenched near
the base of the citadel of Round Top. The other was to keep General [John
B.] Hood from assisting the main Confederate assault on the Union left centre, which [General George G.] Meade expected, and which was in prepara-
tion." General Judson Kilpatrick also hoped to punch a hole through the
rebel defenses in order that he might reach Lee's trains in the Southern rear.
This unfortunate and disastrous assault is sometimes referred to as "Farn-
sworth's Charge," after one of the officers who led it, and who was killed
that day. One of the units involved in this movement was the 1st Vermont,
a cavalry regiment organized in November 1861 and commanded at Gettysburg by Lieutenant Colonel A.W. Preston.

Within the period between four and five o'clock p.m. the 1st Vermont
numbering approximately 680 men came under the concentrated fire of five
Confederate infantry regiments. Their loss was sixty-seven, one of which,

Ira Sparry, was eventually carried to a church in the southeast section of the borough of Gettysburg. While there he was visited often by the mother of Liberty A. Hollinger. The Hollinger family lived northeast of the church at the corner of York Street and the Hanover Road.

In 1925 Liberty narrated the short story of Sparry's last days.

> Mother also visited a young Union soldier by the name of Ira Sparry who lay badly wounded in the [German] Reformed Church. She was much pleased with his general appearance and manners. He seemed to be getting along all right, and when he learned that his wife was comming [sic] to see him he was happy. Their home was in Portland, Maine. She finally arrived and came to our house, but too late to see her husband. He had suddenly taken a turn for the worse, and had died and was buried the day before she reached Gettysburg.

Indeed, this is a brief and of course, sorrowful story. However, it illustrates the fact that most of the approximately 5,400 Northern soldiers killed or mortally wounded in the battle had absolutely nothing written about them to relive their last fleeting minutes or hours on earth. It also points out that as the years passed, important facts about even those men who *were* remembered, could often become hazy and confused. Notice how Hollinger listed his home as Portland when actually Sparry was living in St. Albans, Vermont during the war years.

Corporal Sparry had been wounded by a gunshot of the right thigh on July 3 and the leg was amputated shortly thereafter. His death took place on July 22, 1863. He now rests in the Vermont section of the National Cemetery at Gettysburg.

Privates Ludwig Kreisel and George Kutter,
Battery A, 1st New Jersey Artillery,
4th Volunteer Brigade, Artillery Reserve

This particular segment is the only one in the book which gives the details of the deaths of two men at one time. The reason is due to some confusion which still surrounds the circumstances of the situation. Both soldiers were German artillery privates, both died within minutes of one another, and the witness herein did not distinguish between the two. Here is that unusual drama, as recalled by the battery lieutenant when his unit dashed forward on the afternoon of July 3 to stop the Confederate attack on Cemetery Ridge.

> ...an aide from Gen. [Henry] Hunt came with orders for me to get to the front as quickly as possible....Pickett's division was then advancing....As soon as I got into position the drivers all dismounted, save one. He rode the lead team on the first gun, which was at the right. I sat upon my horse, moving back and forward. The shells from the enemy's guns were bursting over us and all around us. Meanwhile the German driver sat in his saddle as coolly as he would at a table drinking a glass of lager and nibbling a piece of limberger, when a piece of a shell struck him in the side, about the pocket. I was looking right at him at the time. When struck, he raised

in the saddle at least six inches, then settled back, dismounted and stood on his feet for about a second, and then fell. I at once ordered the Sergeant of his detachment to carry him to a tree that was a few yards to the rear and right, and get back to his gun as quickly as possible. The Sergeant did so, but said that he would like to take him to an old house a few rods farther to the rear and right, one that had been used as a hospital in the early part of the day, but at that time fragments of shell and bullets were rattling on the roof like hailstones. I told the Sergeant to take three men and a blanket, carry the wounded man to the house, and do it as quickly as possible and get back to his gun. I do not think the Sergeant and his men were gone more than ten minutes, when he returned and told me that the man was dead, and showed me his pocketbook, dripping with blood, which had been driven by the broken shell partly into his bowels. I opened the book, and as near as I remember there was $20 in bills, which were all stained with blood. The Sergeant told me that the man said that he had no relatives in this country, and that he wanted the Sergeant to take the money and divide it equally among the men of his detachment. I returned the pocketbook to the Sergeant and told him to get to his gun at once.

The next [incident] was at the left gun. I thought the men were working the gun a little slow and rode up pretty close to it, when a shell from the enemy's battery burst in front and slightly above us. A small piece struck my horse, but did no harm. A piece struck an old German soldier, who was number two at the gun. He wheeled around on one foot and fell flat on his back. I jumped from my horse, bent down by him, called him by name. The only audible reply was, "Water." I called for a canteen, placed it to his lips. He took one swallow and was dead. I mounted my horse and ordered the dead man carried to the stone wall (which, as near as I can remember, was not more than 100 feet from my left gun), and covered with a blanket....My battery was on the north side of that, the wall being on my left. The old German soldier that I have just mentioned used to take care of my horses. He was a faithful and good man, and I was truly sorry to see him killed. Just before nightfall, and after the cannonading had ceased, I got the men to dig a grave on the north side of that stone wall. We wrapped the old soldier in his blanket and buried him as tenderly as we could, under the circumstances....

Both artillerymen were buried on the farm of Peter Frey not far from his stone house on the Taneytown Road. Today the men lie in the National Cemetery side by side, just as they fought, in Section A of the New Jersey plot.

Captain John J.P. Blinn, Assistant Adjutant General, 1st Brigade, 2nd Division, 2nd Corps

At the very height of what is now called Pickett's Charge, considered by some a "supreme moment" in American military history, this young captain fell mortally wounded near a small copse of trees along Cemetery Ridge. On July 3, as battered rebel formations hit the wavering Federal defensive

Captain John J.P. Blinn, mortally wounded during the height of combat on July 3, 1863, near the copse of trees or so called "High Water Mark," on Cemetery Ridge.

line, John Blinn was struck by a ball in the hip, nevermore to stand again from the ground he struck moments later. His bone fractured, Blinn was taken to the field hospital of the Second Corps on Jacob Schwartz's farm along Rock Creek. There on July 4 he dictated two letters home, these missives written by a nurse, surgeon, or another soldier at that hospital. The letters arrived in Terre Haute, Indiana, and Blinn's widowed mother made preparations to go to her son.

Meanwhile, an acquaintance of the captain's, Azor Nickerson, 8th Ohio Infantry, who was wounded also but lay in a different area of the same hospital, began an interesting daily ritual. He said of it:

> I then found [from speaking to Reverend Jonathan E. Adams of New Sharon, Maine, a volunteer nurse at the hospital] that my friend was also so badly wounded that it was not thought possible for him to recover...I then sent a message to Blinn, that if I was alive at ten the next morning, I would join him in a glass of wine, at least we could each take one at the same moment.
>
> We continued this long-distance greeting for several mornings until one day just before the time for my glass with Blinn, a message came to my father [who was staying with the recuperating Nickerson]. Instead of opening the bottle of wine for me as had been his custom, he came over by my bunk, laid his hand gently on my forehead, and looking out across the green fields toward the hospital of the Second Division, he said: "Poor Captain Blinn can't drink with you this morning. he is dead."

Fortunately, Blinn's mother, Dorthea, arrived the day before his death, which is remembered by the family as July 14, and shown by his military records to be July 18. She must have shared her son's last desperate moments, and surely made the approaching darkness seem a little brighter.

General William Harrow who commanded the 2nd Division, wrote in part in his report of the Battle of Gettysburg:

...My own assistant adjutant-general, Capt. John P. Blinn, throughout both days manifested himself a thorough soldier and patriot. He fell, mortally wounded, on the 3d, while gallantly cheering on the men of the command to which he was attached. No tribute can now reach him, but a worthier man and soldier has not died for his country.

A second letter posted from Captain Blinn to a woman named "Cora," possibly his betrothed. Nothing more is known of her.

Either the original letter or a family copy of the one sent to Captain Blinn's family from a Second Corps field hospital near Gettysburg. It was probably written by a volunteer nurse or some other person connected with the medical corps.

And in writing to Pastor Lyman Abbott of the Blinn's family church in Terre Haute on September 17, 1863, Reverend J.E. Adams narrated the final days and hours of John Blinn.

My Dear Brother...

On Tues. morning July 7 a surgeon came to me & said he wished a favor. He had been ordered to the front & must go but he felt sadly as he must leave behind a young friend who must die of his wounds. He wished one to care particularly for him & gave me the following instruction.

Inquire for John P. Blinn in the hospital 2nd Corps 2nd Div. His rank is Assistant Adjut. Gen. of Gen. Harrows Staff. I leave $55.50. If he dies before his mother arrives buy coffin. pay for burial in the Cemetery. carefully note the place & write to Mrs. Dorthea Blinn Terre Haute Ind. & enclose Balance of Money if any—Then with tears saying do all you can for Blinn's comfort. he bade me good bye and started—

I went at once to his tent. He was suffering intensely but when I told him his surgeon had sent me to care for him he caught my hand but did not say a word for some minutes. then he said "Surg. tells me I must die. O Lord Jesus have mercy!" I tried calmly to point him to this Jesus speaking of his ability, his willingness, his desire, & his actual effort to save us, all which he readily assented to & expressed his desire to realize it fully—Then I caught the idea of his being from Terre Haute & I ventured an inquiry! "Do you know Rev. Lyman Abbott" "Lyman Abbott! My minister! O how he talked to me the last time I was at home! Do you know him?" I told him how he smile[d] and we were on familiar terms—I saw him very frequently till Friday. I think it was when his mother came. After which I did not see so much of him....

The day before his mother came I was with him a long time. We supposed him sinking. I bade him goodbye and he thought me gone. He closed his eyes as if drowsing with his hands folded upon his breast. As I was just behind him he broke out in ejaculations, & I took note of some of them for his friends sake. First he repeated most of the Hymn—"And crown him Lord of all" Then he said, "Jesus! Jesus! have mercy, have mercy." Then his face seemed so radiant & smiling, as he repeated, "Happy day, since he has washed my sins away"—Then he prayed "Jesus take me to thy house. My mother, sisters, brothers, the Lord bless you all." "O I'm glad salvation's free." "Dear Jesus I come to thee—Jesus, Jesus, Jesus, precious savior."

His good mother can tell you of his last hours. I sympathised [sic] with her as she was in that dismal dying tent, night & day with her noble son. My regards to her if you please & tell her I shall hope to meet her, & her dear son in the world where there is no war, no sorrow, no parting....

After death came, the body was shipped to Indiana where it now rests in the Woodlawn Cemetery of that city.

When Captain John Blinn died he was twenty-three years old and prior to the Civil War had attended Wabash College in Crawfordsville, Indiana. He first joined the 14th Indiana Infantry, serving with that unit until he was appointed to the staff of General Harrow.

*The grave headstone of Captain John Blinn
in Woodlawn Cemetery, Terre Haute, Indiana.*

Corporal Wesley C. Sturtevant, Company E, 14th Vermont Infantry, 3rd Brigade, 3rd Division, 1st Corps

As we have seen, it was not uncommon for officers and men to have thoughts of death or feelings of forthcoming ill-fate prior to battle. A few of these forebodings seemed especially strong and were well documented. This is one of the more detailed stories I have come across, written by the subject's relative, Ralph Sturtevant, 13th Vermont. The following occurred about noon on July 3 along the rear of Cemetery Ridge:

> Just [then]...Corporal Wesley C. Sturtevant...my cousin and playmate from birth to early manhood came from his regiment only a few rods to the left to see me and this is a part of what he said, "I shall never see home and dear friends again, something tells me I shall be slain in this battle, and I cannot drive away the awful thought. I have come to tell you and request that you tell father and mother, brothers and sisters and dear friends for me and say good-by. That I would like to be buried in Weybridge, my native town, that I have done my duty thus far and have not flinched or been much frightened so far in this battle; that when awakened this morning by the roar of cannon and the noise of bursting shell that passed over me, I was dreaming of the consummation of long anticipated joys, and in it I read 'death' and it so impressed me that it is impossible to think of any thing else. I have not felt so until to-day though under fire all day yesterday and many fell dead and wounded about me. I have asked of my Father in Heaven forgiveness for all, and am at peace and all is well, but how I long to live and return home to walk in the path that my desire, hope and ambition had marked out. I am so sure that my life will end on this field that I have come to ask that you explain all to father and mother, take these letters and return them and tell her not to weep for me, that my heart almost breaks to think I must give up all my cherished plans of life. I could not tell these

matters or speak of them to my company comrades, so come to you."

And more he said of like import. In every way I endeavored to dispel the awful thoughts that held and controlled him, but to no purpose. All his life he had listened to the interpretations of his mother's dreams who was a firm believer in such impressions. The author having often heard this sainted mother explain her dreams and knowing of their fulfilment [sic] do not wonder that her oldest child and most beloved son, though educated and intelligent was impressed with the idea that there was some mysterious connection unexplainable between natural and immortal life that revealed to the living premonitions of the future. I cannot forget how anxiously he listened hoping (as I now believe) that some explanation might break the spell that engulfed him. My efforts were all in vain. With deep emotion he extended his hand and said 'Good-by' and hastily and deliberately walked back to his regiment nearby paying no heed to the deadly missiles that filled the air. The author was not a believer in dreams and gave the incident but little thought during the remainder of the day.

Wesley's cousin, Ralph, continued the testimony of the events that transpired after the repulse of Longstreet's assault:

As soon as the battle was over and darkness fell on the field...suddenly the thought flashed on my mind what of my cousin with whom I had the interview just before the cannonading in the afternoon. I wondered now if his premonitions of death had proven a reality. I could not wait and hastened to the 14th to ascertain if dead or alive. Just before reaching his company I met some of his tentmates that were then on their way to find me. They took me only a few steps further and there on the ground as he fell was the mangled body of my cousin W.C. Sturtevant having been shot through the breast by a solid shot or a shell. His comrades told me that he fell just as the regiment rose to take part in the advance against General Pickett's charge, being instantly killed. Only about three hours after his most remarkable conversation and lamentable expressions of premonitions of death on that field. Whatever may be thought concerning warnings of future events, in this case at least there was a perfect fulfilment of what Corporal Sturtevant told me about one o'clock that afternoon. His comrades, Lieut. Andrew J. Childs and others, said that up to the very moment of his death he had showed as much courage and bravery as any one among them, and therefore it was not fear that had awakened and firmly impressed him with death on that field.

On July 4, Ralph Sturtevant was assigned to a burial detail which interred all of the 13th Vermont's "killed in action." These men were buried near a stone wall on a slight elevation just in rear of their battle position on July 3. He said that

Each grave of our comrades buried at Gettysburg was rudely marked with inscription of name of company and regiment and date of death carved on a cartridge box cover or pieces of boards from hard tack boxes that their remains might be found, should occasion require it. The author was with the squad that brought from the field and buried, Corporal Wesley C. Sturtevant....The temporary monument that marked his grave was a cartridge box cover on which I carefully cut with my jack knife, name, company, regiment and date of death, which marker was taken with his remains to his home in Weybridge, Vt., and by his mother affectionately cherished during a long life and by her delivered to me the last time I saw her, which marker is now sacredly cared for as one of the precious mementoes of my army life.

Wesley Sturtevant's temporary grave was near the pump and well belonging to Peter Frey, whose farmhouse stood just in rear of the Vermont brigade's line of battle.

Second Lieutenant Joseph S. Milne, Battery B, 1st Rhode Island Light Artillery, Artillery Brigade, 2nd Corps

Second Lieutenant Joseph S. Milne,
4th United States Artillery.

During the Battle of Gettysburg this officer was attached to Cushing's Battery A, 4th United States Artillery and was in command of the right half sections of the battery. During the Pickett-Pettigrew advance July 3 against the Union left center on Cemetery Ridge, Milne was mortally wounded. This was about the time the Confederates were within two hundred yards of the battery and as its guns fired double and possibly even triple charges of canister into the crumbling gray ranks.

A witness to the precise moment of Lieutenant Milne's death was John B. Linn mentioned earlier as being on leave from the 51st Pennsylvania Infantry, and visiting the battleground. On Wednesday, July 8 Linn and a companion John H. Goodman, after walking over the field, arrived at Cemetery Hill where they inquired for a place they could purchase a meal. The two men were directed to a Mr. Weikel's [or Weikert's] nearby. Here is his recollection of the visit to that house:

> We enquired for something to eat and went into Mr. Weikels and asked and they said they could give us dinner. In the house was Lieut. Jos. S. Milne of Battery "B" Rhode Island Artillery dying from a shot through

the breast. Lieut. Jacob H. Lamb of Battery "A" wounded in the hand was waiting on him. My heart sank within me to see one so young and so fair sinking into the relentless grasp of death. I noticed the nice contents of his hand-trunk looked as if it had been packed by some kind mother. He thought it very hard that he had to die so young. Mr. Bausman was sent for to see him in the afternoon, and his feelings became very much changed. He could not bear Mr. Sweeny out of his sight however. He sank gradually and at 20 min. past two July 9, 1863 he expired with the light of God's mercy shining radiantly down upon him; he was content to die, only desired to see his mother again. He was from Newport, Rhode Island....

Milne's battery commander, Captain John Hazzard recorded these words in his official report: "In his regiment he was noted for his bravery and willingness to encounter death in any guise, while his modesty and manliness gained for him the ready esteem of his many comrades. His death is a loss to all, and we cannot but mourn that so bright a life should thus suddenly be vailed in death."

The uniform coat of 21-year-old Lieutenant Herman Donath, 19th Massachusetts Infantry who fell on July 3, 1863, during Longstreet's afternoon assault. The regimental historian reported: "Lieut. Donath was killed by a buckshot which entered his heart. When found, there was no blood upon his person, but when his clothing was opened, a little round hole was discovered in his side, showing what had caused his death. He was quite boyish looking and in the short time he had been with the company had won its love and respect."

Private Rufus S. Myers,
Company K, 111th New York Infantry,
3rd Brigade, 3rd Division, 2nd Corps

While on the firing line along Cemetery Ridge in the afternoon of July 3, Myers, assisting to repel the assault of Pettigrew's division, received a gunshot wound in the left leg which broke the bone. One of those who nursed him at the U.S. General Hospital was Cornelia Hancock of Philadelphia.

On the day he died, she was writing to a relative:

Camp Letterman, Gen. Hospital
near Gettysburg, Pa.
Aug. 31st, 1863.

My Dear Sister
Those who write to me will get written to. I received thy letter. Today is Sunday. It seems more like one than any that has ever passed since I came here. It is a perfect day. All the men in my ward are doing well but two. Rufus M. is in the process of dying. He belongs to the 111th New York, had keen black eyes and laid in the upper tent where thee saw him. I have taken every care that is possible; was determined to save him, his leg has commenced bleeding and he cannot last long.

Myers did not live through that beautiful August day and was buried the following Monday in Section 6, Grave #24 of the camp graveyard. He now reposes in the National Cemetery, where his black eyes no longer flash, and where his earthly fragments will remain forever.

Private William O. Doubleday, Company H, 14th Vermont Infantry, 3rd Brigade, 3rd Division, 1st Corps

Wounded in the left leg below the knee on July 3, the tibia fractured, Doubleday underwent amputation while in a field hospital located in the Roman Catholic church on High Street in Gettysburg. While there he was visited by the chairman or president of the U.S. Christian Commission, Mr. George H. Stuart, who wrote:

As I was passing, a man near the altar looked up at me imploringly and asked, "Ain't you going to stop and talk to me?" I went to him and ascertained that his name was Wm. O. Doubleday. His wife was a Christian. She had taught each one of his children to pray as soon as they could lisp the words. He had never made a profession of religion himself, but was not what is called a "wicked man."

"When I enlisted," said he, "which I did because I considered it a disgrace to be drafted, just as I was leaving for the war, my wife said, 'I hope you will come back all right, and a good Christian.' It touched my heart. We went into the room with the family, and there she prayed for me, and then asked me to pray. I tried to offer a few broken petitions. My little boy, only thirteen years old, then offered a most earnest prayer for me and for our distressed country. I don't know where he learned to pray like that, unless it was in the Sabbath-school."

When he learned how I was connected with the Commission, and saw the badge, tears came to his eyes. When I spoke to him of Jesus, he pressed my hands, and the tears came fast as rain. I prayed with him, and then he asked me to bend down and kiss him. He died soon after from the effects of an amputation.

I received a letter from his wife, who came to him before his death. She

111

was very earnest in her expressions of thankfulness, and told me with loving sorrow and joy how her husband's peaceful death had answered her prayers.

Private Doubleday, a resident of Sherburne, Vermont, was forty-one when he died August 14, reportably at Camp Letterman, where he was interred in Section 5, Grave #1 the next day. His wife did not choose to carry Doubleday's corpse home, as so many others did, for today it lies in the National Cemetery.

Private Charles M. Lowe,
Company K, 19th Maine Infantry,
1st Brigade, 2nd Division, 11th Corps

Twenty-year-old "Charley" Lowe, an unmarried soldier from Bath, Maine was wounded in the groin, head, and arm about midafternoon of July 3. He was carried to the Jacob Schwartz farm and deposited in that Second Corps hospital on or about July 4, where he lay with several thousand other seriously wounded men until his death on July 12.

A witness to Private Lowe's last words was Reverend R.J. Parvin of the U.S. Christian Commission, who quoted him thus: "Tell mother I received my wound on my twentieth birthday. I give my life for my country; if I had another I would give it too."

Charles Lowe was soon buried in Schwartz's cornfield near Rock Creek which was used as one of the four or five graveyards at this hospital. It is not known if his mother received Reverend Parvin's letter, and his burial place is today also a mystery.

Color Corporal Enoch K. Miller,
Company F, 108th New York Infantry,
2nd Brigade, 3rd Division, 2nd Corps

Colonel Francis E. Pierce witnessed a heartbreaking spectacle just after Pickett's assault on the afternoon of July 3. He explained:

> I saw four of the members of my old company in an ambulance, that came to the front [for the] wounded after the firing had ceased. Miller, [Daniel] Schout, [Darwin] Skinner and [John] Swager. I rode alongside and bade them good bye, I remember how they looked and what they said. One of them said "Good bye Col. they caught me this time," another, "good bye Col be back soon" another "good bye if I dont come back I know that what few are left can take care of our old flags, be careful and not get hit" while poor Enoch Miller could just raise his head and looking very pale and just whisper "good bye Col," and then he gurgled something in his throat that I couldn't understand, and I would not pain him to ask him again what he said. Two of them I did not expect to live an hour, but both I understand are doing well. Such scenes completely unman me. I can stand up and fight, but cannot endure the sight of suffering, particularly of our own men....

The above was written in a letter to Colonel Pierce's friend Edward D. Chapin on July 27, 1863. Corporal Miller, as seen from Pierce's description, understandably could not have survived for long; he is now interred in the National Cemetery at Gettysburg. The good colonel himself, served in the army until 1880. He died in California in 1896. The three other soldiers mentioned by Pierce all survived.

Captain James J. Griffiths,
Company I, 72nd Pennsylvania Infantry,
2nd Brigade, 2nd Division, 2nd Corps

General Oliver O. Howard, commander of the Eleventh Army Corps of the Army of the Potomac published this in a report shortly after the battle: "...I have to report the death of Capt. J.J. Griffiths, aide-de-camp on my staff. He was wounded on the 5th of July, while on a reconnaissance with my body-guard, and died on the 10th of the same month."

The captain, mortally wounded two days *after* the end of the battle, lingered for five days. His situation though, was most unusual. With over 26,000 wounded in and around Gettysburg, the majority suffering in the most primitive conditions possible, he was fortunate enough to have a personal physician assigned to his case. This, when only about one hundred surgeons were detailed to remain in the field hospitals to care for the thousands of anguished and broken bodies of Union and Confederate injured.

The doctor left with Griffiths was Robert Hubbard, formerly of the 17th Connecticut Infantry, who wrote often to his wife. On July 7 he explained his duty to her:

> My own dear Nellie
> You will doubtless be surprised to learn that I have been left behind & that the Army have advanced in pursuit of the enemy. After the terrible fighting on Friday & the complete route of the Rebel Army Genl. Howard's (body guard) with himself and part of his staff thought they would have a little tilt in charging on the rebel picket which they left to keep up appearance & in the fray Capt. Griffith *[sic]* of the staff was seriously wounded & Genl. Howard requested me to remain with him until out of danger....

An eyewitness reported that the captain was taken to a private residence in Gettysburg, where he was visited one last time by his friend and commander:

> As the Army of the Potomac was preparing to move in pursuit of Lee, General Howard rode to the door. Dismounting, an orderly took his horse, whilst the General passed in to the side of the dying man. The two had loved each other as brothers. Howard clasped the Captain in his arms, kissed him and burst into a flood of tears.
> Recovering his self-possession, the Christian General took from his pocket a testament and read to the dying Captain a portion of the fourteenth chapter of St. John's gospel....

The General then knelt down and offered up a fervent and impressive prayer. Arising from his knees, he again kissed the dying man, saying, "We shall meet in heaven."

Doctor Hubbard, who was boarding on Baltimore Street at the house of Drs. William Taylor and James Cress, and where Captain Griffiths may have been quartered also, continued to stay in touch with his spouse, Nellie. On the 9th of July he penned: "Capt. Griffith, my patient is no better & still in a critical condition so that I cannot tell how long I may be detained here. I am very anxious to rejoin the corps and hope a favorable change in his condition may release me soon."

Friday, July 10, 1863 brought this:

> I am still here and confined all the time to the house with Capt. Griffith. Yesterday I did not think he would live until this morning but is now a little better tho. with little prospect of recovery. I visit the Genl Hospital daily but the Capt. is unwilling that I should stay long so that I cannot do as much there as I wish.

> Saturday morning (July 11) 8 oclk
> I am sorry darling that this letter was too late for mail yesterday but the trains are irregular. Poor Capt. Griffith died at 12 o'clock last night and I am busy arranging to send his body to Phila. He was a brave fellow but has fought his last battle. I have seen over him almost constantly since last Sunday and am very tired but shall probably leave to join the Corps tomorrow....
>
> > Yours loving husband
> > R. Hubbard

On July 14, the doctor parted from Gettysburg for Baltimore with a train of five hundred wounded, including Captain Frederick W. Stowe, Harriet Beecher Stowe's son, who had been wounded by a piece of shell on July 3 near General O.O. Howard's headquarters on Cemetery Hill.

Private Lewis Dellair, Company C, 125th New York Infantry, 3rd Brigade, 3rd Division, 2nd Corps

As has been noted previously, not all of the men who fell in the Gettysburg Campaign died through the conventional ways most often associated with a great battle or military campaign. For example, at the beginning of this book the first story depicted was that of a soldier named Clark who died as a result of sunstroke.

The ensuing diary quoted, kept by Private Charles W. Belknap portrays an equally unusual death some five days after the Battle of Gettysburg. While following up R.E. Lee's retreating Confederate army, Belknap wrote:

> Wed., July 8, 1863—We marched to within four miles of Frederick City through Brookville and Woodsburg. It rained hard nearly all this forenoon and we had to march through a great deal of mud. About noon a man by

the name of Lanshaw *[sic]* of Co. C accidently shot his comrade Lewis Dellair with an old horse pistol which he had found but didn't know it was loaded. The ball went through his head and he died almost instantly. He was buried on the spot. Today we heard with joy of the fall of Vicksburg.

A good prospect exists that somewhere in the vicinity of the old villages of Brookville and Woodsburg (towns no longer listed on a contemporary map of Maryland) lies the long lost grave of Private Dellair. Fate decided that he should survive the terrible three days at Gettysburg, only to be cut down in the flower of youth by a simple case of pure misfortune.

The soldier who accidentally killed Dellair was possibly John C. Lambert or Thomas Lineham.

Captain Charles Mortimer Wheeler, Company K, 126th New York Infantry. At the time of his death, Captain Wheeler was on the advance skirmish line of General Alexander Hays' Division near the Emmitsburg Road just west of Abraham Brien's farm buildings. He was killed on the morning of July 3 by a Confederate sharpshooter posted in the William Bliss barn, and was later buried on Cemetery Ridge in a grove owned by David Ziegler. Wheeler was born in Canandaigua, New York on December 8, 1837. He was practicing law in that village when the war began in 1861, having attended Yale College several years earlier. Today he lies in the graveyard of the Congregational Church at Canandaigua. The poem printed in the Epilogue of this book was written as a tribute to Captain Wheeler.

Unknown Union Soldier,
Company, Regiment, Brigade, and
Division also unknown.

It did not seem right to ignore the hundreds and hundreds of Federal soldiers who lost their lives at Gettysburg and were never identified. Many accounts I researched mentioned the deaths of men, some in great detail, but these sources chose or were unable to furnish the name of the casualty. Here then is one such history as told by a volunteer nurse, Mary Cadwell Fisher of York, Pennsylvania. Mrs. Fisher, who did service in the Second Corps hospital, remembered a youth she met on or about July 6:

> One beautiful evening, after a long day's hard work, one of my boys came to me and said: "There is a little chap out there who heard there was a woman from his home and he wants to see you." I found him at the farthest extremity of the hospital, with a half dozen other hopeless cases. He was a lovely boy, scarcely more than a child, who had run away from his home in Providence, Rhode Island, to join the "drum corps." He was a brave boy and a great pet among the soldiers, who nursed him as tenderly as possible, but could poorly supply a mother's loving care. How he longed for one more look of her dear face and once again to hear her sweet words of love. He was so frail and slight it was a marvel how he could have endured the fatigue and privation so long. He was not disfigured by wounds, but constant marches, insufficient food and often sleepless nights had exhausted his strength and he had not vitality to resist the sharp attack of fever. He was perfectly conscious, but too weak to say much.
>
> I asked the poor child what I could do for him. "Oh, I want my mother!" I sat down on the ground and taking him in my arms tried to comfort him. He turned his face to me, saying, "I am so tired," laid his head against me and appeared to sleep. The last rays of the sun touched the lovely features of the dying boy. The long drawn shadows vanished in the gathering darkness. Silence, unbroken save by the plaintive moan of some poor victim, succeeded the hum of the busy day. The pitying dews shed a balm upon his brow. Fainter and fainter grew the breath and more feeble the clasp of the little hand, when, suddenly rousing, he opened his eyes, glazed in death, and looking long and earnestly in my face, said: "Kiss me, lady before I die!" Clinging still closer to the stranger who could but faintly represent the fond mother's tenderness he so eagerly craved, he dropped his heavy eyelids and slept away his brief life as peacefully as a child goes to sleep in its mother's arms. I gently laid the lifeless form down on the hard earth and left him to a soldier's burial and a nameless grave. Poor fellow, what an atom he seemed to be in all that mass of wretched, suffering, dying humanity! Yet he was all the world to the heart of that mother, who wept and prayed for her darling's safe return to the distant home, that never again would echo his boyish step or ringing laugh.

Possibly somewhere in the National Cemetery at Gettysburg the remains of this young musician sleeps, and his epitaph shall read:

Here Rests In
Honored Glory
An American
Soldier
Known But To God.

Epilogue

For the person who has carefully read the previous biographies of 100 Union soldiers who fell at Gettysburg, certain questions must naturally arise: Why did they die and others did not? What was the reason for their deaths? What was accomplished?

One writer, a former member of the 4th Michigan Infantry, L.H. Salsbury, gave serious thought to those questions and attempted an answer in a speech recited to a gathering of veterans at Gettysburg in 1889.

Before this war men called statesmen, standing in the high places of the earth, declared that the Union was a rope of sand, a mere partnership of States, from which any State had a right to withdraw at pleasure. Amid the whirlpool of death on this sacred field you sounded the death knell of that sentiment, and pointed the idea of an imperishable union with bayonets, loaded it with powder and ball, and sealed it forever with your blood. No sane man will ever again declare that this nation has no power of self-preservation, no power to coerce a State. Secession will never again rear its horrid front in this land. At last we are a nation of free men, with common interests, a common purpose and a common destiny.[8]

A second soldier, a New Jersey veteran, who was somewhat more direct, and not quite as eloquent, said in the same year:

[After the Battle of Gettysburg] we passed over the new-made graves, where Southern soldiers had left the bones of their comrades from Virginia, North Carolina and Texas. Yet they had wasted their lives and shed their blood in vain. The star of the Confederacy waned the day they fell. The brilliant illusion was broken, and Southern independence was impossible.[9]

Northern graves too, naturally lay scattered across the forelorn landscape surrounding historic Gettysburg. There were 3,556 combat-related deaths there, 1,697 of them unknown. All would soon be moved to, and be honored within, the Soldier's National Cemetery. Total Federal deaths associated with the Gettysburg Campaign would easily reach upwards of between 5,100 and 5,400.[10] It was a fearful price to pay to save the Union, a Union which had been forged in battle by the forefathers of some of these men. But they paid the price— reluctantly of course, and they paid in full.

"And who has forgotten that gifted youth, who fell on the memorable field of Gettysburg? To win a noble name, to save a beloved country, he took his place beneath the dear old flag, and while cannon thundered and sabers clashed and the stars of the old Union shone above his head he went down in the shock of battle and left us desolate, a name to love and a glory to endure. And as we solemnly know, as by the old charter of liberty we most sacredly swear, he was truly and faithfully and religiously

> Of all our friends the noblest,
> The choicest and the purest,
> The nearest and the dearest,
> In the field at Gettysburg.

> Of all the heroes bravest,
> Of soul the brightest, whitest,
> Of all the warriors greatest,
> Shot dead at Gettysburg.

> And where the fight was thickest,
> And where the smoke was blackest,
> And where the fire was hottest,
> On the fields of Gettysburg,

> There flashed his steel the brightest,
> There blazed his eyes the fiercest,
> There flowed his blood the reddest
> On the field of Gettysburg.

> O wailing winds of heaven!
> O weeping dew of evening!
> O music of the waters
> That flow at Gettysburg,
> Mourn tenderly the hero,
> The rare and glorious hero,
> The loved and peerless hero,
> Who died at Gettysburg.

> His turf shall be the greenest,
> His roses bloom the sweetest,
> His willow droop the saddest
> Of all at Gettysburg.
> His memory live the freshest,
> His fame be cherished longest,
> Of all the holy warriors,
> Who fell at Gettysburg.

These were patriots, these were our jewels. When shall we see their like again?"[11]

Notes

1. Patterson, W.J. *Pennsylvania at Gettysburg*. vol. I, Harrisburg, PA: Wm. Stanley Ray, State Printer, p. 385.

2. Ibid.

3. Keesy, W.A. *WAR—As Viewed From The Ranks*. Norwalk, NY: The Experiment and News Co., 1898, p. 166.

4. Morhous, Henry C. *Reminiscences of the 123d Regiment, N.Y.S.V.*....Greenwich, NY: Peoples Journal Book and Job Office, 1879, p. 53.

5. Haley, John W. *The Rebel Yell & Yankee Hurrah*. Ed. by Ruth L. Silliker. Camden, ME: Down East Books, 1985, p. 106.

6. Judson, Amos M. *History of the Eighty-third Regiment Pennsylvania Volunteers*. Erie, PA: B.F.H. Lynn, Publisher, 1865, p. 134.

7. Conwell, Russell H. *Magnolia Journey*. Ed. by Joseph C. Carter, University, AL: University of Alabama Press, 1974, p. 183.

8. Monument Commission. *Michigan At Gettysburg*. Detroit, MI: Winn & Hammond, 1889, p. 83.

9. Haines, Alanson A. *History of the Fifteenth Regiment New Jersey Volunteers*. New York: Jenkins & Thomas, printers, 1883, p. 96.

10. Busey, John W. *The Last Full Measure*. Hightstown, NJ: Longstreet House, 1988, p. XXIX.

Busey, John W. *These Honored Dead*. Hightstown, NJ: Longstreet House, 1988, p. 6.

11. Richards, Caroline C. *Village Life in America*. Williamstown, MA: Corner House Publishers, 1972, p. 153.

"They made a speech, and played a trumpet and
dressed me in a uniform and then they killed me."
Irwin Shaw

Bibliographical Notes
Part I

Private Robert H. Clark, 7th Maine Infantry
Frederic S. Klein. *Just South of Gettysburg.* Westminster, MD: The Newman Press, 1963, p. 108.

Corporal Wilson D. Race, 149th Pennsylvania Infantry
Elizabeth Salome Myers Stewart, "Reminiscences of Gettysburg Hospitals," unpublished manuscript written in the 1870s and now in the Adams County Historical Society, Gettysburg, PA. Mrs. Stewart's husband, Dr. Henry F. Stewart, died in 1868 and she returned to the profession of teaching. Her sisters were Susan M. Myers who died in 1924 and Jennie Myers Tawney who also died in that year.

Corporal Joseph B. Ruhl, 150th Pennsylvania Infantry
Thomas Chamberlain. *History of the One Hundred and Fiftieth Regiment Pennsylvania Volunteers....* Philadelphia, PA: J.B. Lippincott Co., 1895, p. 155.

Sergeant Alexander M. Stewart, 149th Pennsylvania Infantry
Elizabeth S.M. Stewart, "Gettysburg's Memories Of Its Terrible Fourth," newspaper interview, author not cited, *North American,* July 4, 1909, Philadelphia, PA.

Sergeant Major Asa W. Blanchard, 19th Indiana Infantry
Henry C. Marsh, "The Nineteenth Indiana at Gettysburg," unpublished memoir in the Indiana State Library, Indianapolis, IN.

Private James C. Perrine, 2nd Wisconsin Infantry
Sophronia E. Bucklin. *In Hospital and Camp:....* Philadelphia, PA: John E. Potter and Company, 1869, p. 181.

Private Louis Gardner, 19th Indiana Infantry
George A. Otis, Surgeon General, Army Medical Museum, vol. 3, specimen #1956, photograph #104, Washington, D.C.

Private Levi Stedman, 6th Wisconsin Infantry
Horatio B. Hackett. *Christian Memorials of the War.* Boston, MA: Gould and Lincoln, 1864, p. 132.
William Beaudot and Lance Herdegen. *In the Bloody Railroad Cut at Gettysburg.* Dayton, OH: Morningside Bookshop, 1990, p. 192.
Rufus R. Davis. *Service with the Sixth Wisconsin Volunteers.* Dayton, OH: Press of Morningside Bookshop, 1984, p. 168.

Private Stephen C. Crofut, 17th Connecticut Infantry
J. Henry Blakeman, unpublished letter in the collection of Lewis Leigh, Jr., Fairfax, VA.

Corporal William Egolf, 84th New York Infantry
William F. Howard. *The Gettysburg Death Roster.* Dayton, OH: Morningside House, 1990, p. 56.

Corporal John Walls, 24th Michigan Infantry
George Duffield, Jr., letter published in *Advertiser and Tribune,* Detroit, MI, July 31, 1863.

Private Amos P. Sweet, 150th Pennsylvania Infantry
Elizabeth S.M. Stewart, "Reminiscences of Gettysburg Hospitals," op. cit.
Elizabeth S.M. Stewart, "How A Gettysburg Schoolteacher Spent Her Vacation in 1863," article, *Sunday Call,* San Francisco, CA, August 16, 1903.

Private James M. Daniel, 27th Pennsylvania Infantry
J. Howard Wert, "In the Hospitals of Gettysburg," Harrisburg, PA, *Telegraph,* July 2-October 7, 1907, # 9.

Private Theodore A. Weaver, 153rd Pennsylvania Infantry
W.H.D. Hatton and Carleton A. Shurtleff, letter in the private collection of Randall Hackenburg, Carlisle, PA.

Captain Stephen C. Whitehouse, 16th Maine Infantry
Abner R. Small. *The Road to Richmond.* Berkeley, CA: University of California Press, 1939, p. 98.

Maine Commissioners. *Maine at Gettysburg.* Portland, ME: The Lakeside Press, 1898, p. 68.

Sergeant Christian Taifel, 107th Ohio Infantry
Alfred Rider, letter in the Batchelder Papers at the Gettysburg National Military Park library, Gettysburg, PA.

Private Albion B. Mills, 16th Maine Infantry
Anna M. Holstein. *Three Years in Field Hospitals of the Army of the Potomac.* Philadelphia, PA: J.B. Lippincott & Co., 1867, p. 45.

Private Daniel H. Purdy, 17th Connecticut Infantry
Report of the General Agent of the State of New York. Albany, NY: Comstock & Cassidy Printers, 1864, p. 44.

Private John Flye, 13th Massachusetts Infantry
Austin C. Stearns. *Three Years with Company K.* Arthur A. Kent, editor. Cranbury, NJ: Fairleigh Dickinson University Press, 1976, p. 189.

Sergeant Samuel Comstock, 17th Connecticut Infantry
Justus M. Silliman. *A New Canaan Private in the Civil War.* Edward Marcus, editor. New Canaan, CT: New Canaan Historical Society, 1984, p. 33-48; also Silliman's unpublished letters in the NCHS's collection.

Lieutenant Colonel George Arrowsmith, 157th New York Infantry
John Applegate. *Reminiscences and Letters of George Arrowsmith of New Jersey.* Red Bank, NJ: 1913, p. 211-217.
Captain Adams, who showed Dr. Arrowsmith the grave of his brother, died on July 25 of wounds received in the battle.

Color Sergeant Henry G. Brehm, 149th Pennsylvania Infantry
John H. Bassler, "The Color Episode of the 149th Pennsylvania Volunteers," (1907), *Confederate Veteran* Magazine, vol. 37, 1909, p. 266.
John H. Bassler, "Reminiscences of the First Day's Fight at Gettysburg," an address delivered at Albright Collegiate Institute, PA, June, 1895, p. 7.

Color Sergeant Lewis Bishop, 154th New York Infantry
Report of the General Agent of the State of New York. Albany, NY: Comstock & Cassidy Printers, 1864, p. 46.
F.J.F. Schantz. *Reflections on the Battle of Gettysburg.* R.S. Shay, editor. Lebanon County Historical Society, PA, vol. XIII, no. 6, 1963, p. 295.
Emory Sweetland, letters in the files of the Gettysburg National Military Park library and in the collection of Lyle Sweetland.

Private John Aeigle, 107th Ohio Infantry
Justus M. Silliman, *A New Canaan Private in the Civil War,* op. cit., p. 45.

Private James Gillen, 11th Pennsylvania Infantry
William T. Simpson, "The Drummer Boys of Gettysburg," Philadelphia, PA, *North American,* June 29, 1913, p. 2.

Part II

Corporal John Ackerman, 82nd Illinois Infantry
Illinois Infantry file at Gettysburg National Military Park library. See article entitled, "History of the Jews of Chicago."
Private Albert H. Frost, 3rd Maine Infantry
"Burial Notes" file in author's collection.
Samuel B. Wing. *The Soldier's Story.* Phillips, ME: Phonograph print, 1898.
Sergeant George F. Spear, 3rd Maine Infantry
Harmon Martin letter in the archives of the United Daughters of the Confederacy, Madison, GA, Chapter.
Maine Commissioners, *Maine at Gettysburg,* op. cit., p. 143.
Private Timothy Kearns, 71st New York Infantry
Joseph H. Twitchell, letter written to his sister, July 5, 1863, now in the Yale University Library, New Haven, CT.
Sergeant Henry L. Richards, Co. F, 2nd United States Sharpshooters
Wyman S. White. *The Civil War Diary of....* Edited and privately printed by Lieutenant Colonel Russell C. White, U.S.M.C. (Retired).
Sergeant Richards was 37 years old and from Portsmouth, NH. He is one of the few cases this writer has ever uncovered who died of an overdose of, or by the misuse of, ether or chloroform. However, it is believed that many such examples occurred, the blame for these deaths was usually attributed to other causes.
Captain John M. Sell, 83rd Pennsylvania Infantry
Amos M. Judson. *History of the Eighty-Third Regiment Pennsylvania Volunteers.* Erie, PA: B.F.H. Lynn, publisher, 1865, p. 133.
Corporal John Scott, 124th New York Infantry
New York Monuments Commission. *New York at Gettysburg,* vol. II. Albany, NY: J.B. Lyon Company, 1900, p. 871.
Private Thomas H. Hunt, 44th New York Infantry
Eugene A. Nash. *A History of the Forty-Fourth Regiment New York Volunteer Infantry.* Chicago, IL: The Lakeside Press, R.R. Donnelley & Sons Company, 1910, p. 324.
Mark Hunt, "The Legacy I Leave," an account of his life, 1839-1899, privately printed. My thanks to William A. Frassanito for his kindness in providing this excellent source.
Sergeant George W. Buck, 20th Maine Infantry
Maine Commissioners, *Maine at Gettysburg,* op. cit., p. 268.
Joshua L. Chamberlain, "Through Blood and Fire at Gettysburg," *Hearst's Magazine,* vol. 23, #6, June, 1913, p. 904.
George Buck was reduced to the rank of private during the winter of 1862-63 when he, as a sergeant, refused to cut firewood for the regimental quartermaster. Buck, also sick at the time, was charged with insubordination, a situation he could not defend against since there were no witnesses to the incident. The regiment as a whole was greatly displeased at this action.
First Lieutenant Eugene L. Dunham, 44th New York Infantry
Eugene A. Nash, *A History of the Forty-Fourth Regiment New York Volunteer Infantry in the Civil War,* op. cit., p. 295.
One other source stated that Dunham was hit in the right temple.

The stone Bricker farmhouse where Dunham was buried still sits along the Taneytown Road just a few miles south of Gettysburg.

Private James Johnston, 4th Michigan Infantry
James Houghton, unpublished private journal, at the Library of the University of Michigan, Ann Arbor, MI.

Second Lieutenant Franklin K. Garland, 61st New York Infantry
Charles A. Fuller. *Personal Recollections of the War of 1861.* Reprint. Hamilton, NY: Edmonston Publishing, Inc., 1990, p. 101. Also newspaper article in the *Sherburne News,* October 20, 1906, kindly provided by Herb Crumb, Norwich, NY. Gregory A. Coco. *A Vast Sea of Misery: A History and Guide to the Union and Confederate Field Hospitals at Gettysburg.* Gettysburg, PA: Thomas Publications, 1988. For limited information available on the "Bair" farm, see p. 89; for the "Weikert" farm, see p. 68.

Corporal David C. Laird, 4th Michigan Infantry
Horatio G. Jones. *To the Christian Soldiers and Sailors of the Union....* Philadelphia, PA: Lippincott's Press, 1868, p. 166.
Jacob Shenkel, 1863, diary in the possession of Timothy Brooks, E. Liverpool, OH, p. 22.

Private Rowland L. Ormsby, 64th New York Infantry
Emily B.T. Souder. *Leaves from the Battle-field of Gettysburg.* Philadelphia, PA: Caxton Press, 1864, p. 53.

Private Charles F. Gardner, 110th Pennsylvania Infantry
St. Clair A. Mulholland. *The Story of the 116th Regiment Pennsylvania Volunteers....*Philadelphia, PA: F. McManus, Jr., & Co., 1903, p. 138.

Private William L. Purbeck, 5th Massachusetts Light Artillery
Luther E. Cowles. *History of the 5th Massachusetts Battery.* Boston, MA: L.E. Cowles, publisher, 1902, p. 640.

Private John Buckley, 140th Pennsylvania Infantry
Robert L. Stewart. *History of the One Hundred and Fortieth Regiment Pennsylvania Volunteers.* Published by the Regimental Association, 1912, p. 424.
The woman who married Lieutenant Purman, later Doctor Purman, Mary Witherow, lived on Baltimore St. in Gettysburg with her parents, Eliza and Samuel Witherow.

First Lieutenant Horatio F. Lewis, 145th Pennsylvania Infantry
John H.W. Stuckenberg, unpublished diary in the Musselman Library of Gettysburg College. Used with the kind permission of David T. Hendrick, Special Collections Librarian, who has generously transcribed and edited the document.

Private William Chamberlain, 141st Pennsylvania Infantry
John D. Bloodgood. *Personal Reminiscences of the War.* New York, NY: Hunt & Eaton, 1893, p. 150.

Second Lieutenant Benjamin R. Wright, 26th Pennsylvania Infantry
John B. Linn, "Journal of my trip to the battlefield at Gettysburg," p. 13, Centre County Library, Bellefonte, PA.

Sergeant William S. Jordan, 20th Maine Infantry
Horatio B. Hackett. *Christian Memorials of the War.* Boston, MA: Gould and Lincoln, 1864, p. 125.

Private Alvin L. Greenlee, 140th Pennsylvania Infantry
Matilda "Tillie" Pierce Alleman. *At Gettysburg....* NY: W. Luke Borland, 1889, p. 110.

Private James H. McCleary, 1st Pennsylvania Reserve Artillery
Charles S. Wainwright. *A Diary of Battle.* NY: Harcourt, Brace & World, Inc., 1962, p. 243.
Private Solan L. Cornell, 17th U.S. Infantry
J.P. Hackett, "The Fifth Corps At Gettysburg," article, *National Tribune,* July 29, 1915.
Sergeant Major Charles Ward, 32nd Massachusetts Infantry
Francis J. Parker. *The Story of the 32nd Regiment Massachusetts Infantry.* Boston, MA: C.W. Calkins & Co., 1880, p. 173.
Colonel Charles F. Taylor, 42nd Pennsylvania Infantry
Aaron Baker, letter published in *The Pennsylvania Magazine of History and Biography,* July, 1973.
Board of Commissioners, *Pennsylvania At Gettysburg,* vol. I, op. cit., p. 30.
Second Lieutenant Robert E. Evans, 108th New York Infantry
Francis M. Wafer, unpublished diary at the Douglas Library, Queen's University, Kingston, Ontario, Canada.
Theron E. Parson, diary entry, July 2, 1863, copy in Gettysburg National Military Park library.
Private Cyrus Plumer, 62nd Pennsylvania Infantry
Letters, photos and other sources in the private collection of David Neville of Export, PA, 15632.
Jacob Shenkel, diary, op. cit., p. 25.
Colonel Edward E. Cross, 5th New Hampshire Infantry
William Child, M.D. *A History of the Fifth Regiment New Hampshire Volunteers....* Bristol, NH: R.W. Musgrove, printer, 1893, p. 211.
Thomas L. Livermore. *Days and Events, 1860-1866.* Boston, MA: Houghton Mifflin Co., 1920, p. 254.
Charles A. Hale, "With Colonel Cross at the Wheatfield," Harrisburg, PA: *Civil War Times Illustrated,* vol. XIII, #5, 1974, p. 30.
J.W. Muffly, editor. *The Story of Our Regiment.* Des Moines, IA: Kenyon Printing and Mfg. Co., 1904, p. 173, 244 and 461.
The lieutenant mentioned by Livermore was indeed Charles W. Patch, a 31-year-old Portsmouth, NH man, who was wounded in the abdomen and died on July 10.
Major Israel P. Spalding, 141st Pennsylvania Infantry
David Craft. *History of the One Hundred Forty-First Regiment, Pennsylvania Volunteers, 1862-1865.* Towanda, PA: Reporter-Journal Printing, Co., 1885, p. 128.
Captain Robert M. Forster, 148th Pennsylvania Infantry
Board of Commissioners, *Pennsylvania At Gettysburg,* vol. II, op. cit., p. 732.
J.M. Muffly, editor, *The Story of Our Regiment,* op. cit., p. 245 and 577.
John B. Linn, diary, op. cit., p. 12.
Captain Joseph A. Hubbard, 2nd New Hampshire Infantry
Martin A. Haynes. *History of the Second Regiment, New Hampshire Volunteers....* Manchester, NH: Charles F. Livingston, printer, 1865, p. 182.
The Confederate officer was Colonel Joseph Wasden, 22nd Georgia. For an account of his burial, see Gregory A. Coco. *Wasted Valor: The Confederate Dead at Gettysburg.* Gettysburg, PA: Thomas Publications, 1990, p. 143.
Private Samuel Spear, 42nd Pennsylvania Infantry
O.R. Howard Thompson and William H. Rauch. *History of the "Bucktails."* Dayton,

OH: Morningside House, Inc., p. 268.

Second Lieutenant Isaac A. Dunsten, 105th Pennsylvania Infantry
Anna M. Holstein. *Three Years in Field Hospitals of the Army of the Potomac,* op. cit., p. 48.

Private Erastus A. Allen, 145th Pennsylvania Infantry
John H.W. Stuckenberg, unpublished diary, op. cit., p. 23.

Private John Edmonds, 1st Ohio Light Artillery
Justus M. Silliman, *A New Canaan Private in the Civil War,* op. cit., p. 45.

Second Lieutenant Amaziah J. Barber, 11th U.S. Infantry
George R. Bliss, unpublished letter in the collection of Lewis Leigh, Jr., of Fairfax, VA.

Second Lieutenant Silas A. Miller, 12th U.S. Infantry
B.P. Mimmack, letter on file in the Gettysburg National Military Park library.
Edmund J. Raus, Jr. *A Generation on the March—The Union Army at Gettysburg.* Lynchburg, VA: H.E. Howard, Inc., 1987, p. 154.

Private William Walton, 155th Pennsylvania Infantry
Porter John T., *Under the Maltese Cross....* (Pittsburgh, PA: 155th Regimental Association, 1910), p. 194.

Corporal Samuel M. Caldwell, 118th Pennsylvania Infantry
Author Unknown, "Scenes and Incidents at Gettysburg," *Harper's Weekly,* January 16, 1864.
John L. Smith. *History of 118th Pennsylvania (Corn Exchange) Volunteers....* Philadelphia, PA: J.L. Smith, 1888, p. 251.
John W. Busey. *These Honored Dead.* Hightstown, NJ: Longstreet House, 1988, p. 221. An officer of the 118th, either Captain Charles Fernald or Lieutenant A.H. Walters wrote in a letter dated July 2, 1863, "Owing to our fine position when engaged we lost but one man killed in our company, Corporal Caldwell."

Private Charles F. Howard, 2nd New Hampshire Infantry
Mrs. J. Paxton Bigham, "The Scotts and Cunninghams See the Battle," *Gettysburg Times,* PA, April 22, 1941.

Private Martin J. Coleman, 5th Massachusetts Light Artillery
Luther E. Cowles, *History of the Fifth Massachusetts Battery,* op. cit., p. 659.
The Trostle farm was legally owned by Abraham's father, Peter.

Second Lieutenant William J. Cockburn, 120th New York Infantry
Theodore B. Gates. *The Ulster Guard and the War of the Rebellion.* New York, NY: Benjamin H. Tyrrel, 1879, p. 460.

Private Jonathan E. Leavitt, 12th New Hampshire Infantry
Mary D. Musgrove. Autobiography of Captain Richard W. Musgrove. Published by the author, 1921, p. 93.

Private Augustus Koenig, 1st Minnesota Infantry
Charles Muller, from a personal history written after the war and now in the possession of the Minnesota Historical Society, St. Paul, MN.

Private Hushai C. Thomas, 19th Maine Infantry
Emily B.T. Souder, *Leaves from the Battle-field of Gettysburg,* op. cit., p. 64.

Corporal William C. Schultz, 71st Pennsylvania Infantry
Anna M. Holstein, *Three Years in Field Hospitals of the Army of the Potomac,* op. cit., p. 45.

Private Patrick J. Lannegan, 1st Rhode Island Light Artillery

Thomas M. Aldrich. *The History of Battery A in the War To Preserve The Union.* Providence, RI: Snow & Farnham, printers, 1904, p. 220.

Private Ernest Simpson, 1st Rhode Island Light Artillery
George Lewis. *The History of Battery E, First Regiment Rhode Island Light Artillery....* Providence, RI: Snow & Farnham, printers, 1892, p. 210.

Private James H. Riggin, 1st Pennsylvania Light Artillery
Board of Commissioners, *Pennsylvania at Gettysburg,* vol. I, op. cit., p. 922.
A Confederate officer killed among the guns that night was Lieutenant Louis Worcester, 7th Louisiana Infantry, a lawyer from Baton Rouge.

Part III

Corporal James O. Butcher, 28th Pennsylvania Infantry
William T. Simpson, *The Drummer Boys of Gettysburg,* op. cit., p. 3.

Private Erastus B. Roberts, 84th New York Infantry
George K. Collins. *Memoirs of the 149th Regiment New York Volunteer Infantry....* Syracuse, NY: published by the author, 1891, p. 144.

Captain Thomas B. Fox, 2nd Massachusetts Infantry
Harvard Memorial Biographies, vol. II. Cambridge, MA: Sever and Francis, 1866, p. 122.
Everette W. Pattison. *War Papers and Personal Reminiscences.* Military Order of the Loyal Legion, Missouri Chapter, p. 263.

Private John Costello, 5th U.S. Artillery
William T. Simpson, *The Drummer Boys of Gettysburg,* op. cit., p. 4.

Private Gustavus Ritter, 111th New York Infantry
Samuel B. McIntyre, letter in the Batchelder Papers at the Gettysburg National Military Park library.

Private Alfred G. Gardner, 1st Rhode Island Light Artillery
John H. Rhodes. *The History of Battery B, First Regiment Rhode Island Light Artillery in the War....* Providence, RI: Snow & Farnham, printers, 1894, p. 209.

Sergeant George O. Fell, 143rd Pennsylvania Infantry
J. Howard Wert, "In the Hospitals of Gettysburg," op. cit., # 12.

Corporal Alfred G. Ryder, 1st Michigan Cavalry
Chaplain William C. Way, 24th Michigan Infantry, letters published in various Detroit, MI newspapers between July 7 and August 14, 1863.
Alfred G. Ryder, John G. Frey, Alfred Noble, and William C. Way, unpublished letters in the collection of the University of Michigan, Ann Arbor, MI.

Captain George C. Thompson, 69th Pennsylvania Infantry
Editorial of the Cincinnati *Enquirer* at the 50th Anniversary of the Battle of Gettysburg, *Confederate Veteran* Magazine, #21, 1913, p. 383.
Pennsylvania Daily Telegraph, Harrisburg, PA, notice printed on July 10, 1863.

Private James T. Bedell, 7th Michigan Cavalry
Text and photo are courtesy of the Otis Historical Archives, vol. I, National Museum of Health and Medicine, Washington, D.C., Michael Rhode, Archivist.

Captain Ephraim Wood, 125th New York Infantry
New York Monuments Commission. *New York at Gettysburg,* vol. II. Albany, NY: J.B. Lyon Company, printers, 1900, p. 890.
Charles W. Belknap, unpublished diary in the files of the Gettysburg National Military Park library.

Private Frederick Corcelins, 5th Michigan Cavalry
Edward Corcelins, unpublished letters at the University of Michigan, Ann Arbor, MI.
Corporal Adon G. Wills, 72nd Pennsylvania Infantry
Frank Moore. *Woman of the War.* Hartford, CT: S.S. Scranton & Co., 1867, p. 159.
Corporal Ira E. Sparry, 1st Vermont Cavalry
Liberty A. Hollinger. *The Battle of Gettysburg.* Privately printed, 1925, edited by Elsie Singmaster, p. 11.
G.G. Benedict. *Vermont in the Civil War, A History,* vol. II. Burlington, VT: The Free Press Association, 1888, p. 597.
Privates Ludwig Kreisel and George Kutter, 1st New Jersey Artillery
Augustine N. Parsons, letter written from Summit, Tyler County, TX, June 2, 1889; copy in author's file.
Captain John J.P. Blinn, AAG, 1st Brigade, 2nd Division, 2nd Corps
John J.P. Blinn, July 4, 1863 original letters and photographs in the author's collection.
Jonathan E. Adams, original letter, September 17, 1863, to Lyman Abbott in author's collection.
Official Record of the War of the Rebellion, Washington, D.C., US Government Printing Office, 1889, vol. 27, Part I, p. 421.
Azor H. Nickerson, "Personal Recollections of Two Visits To Gettysburg," *Scribner's Magazine,* vol. XIV, New York, NY, 1893, p. 25. Blinn's father had died several years before the war in a hunting accident.
Corporal Wesley C. Sturtevant, 14th Vermont Infantry
Ralph O. Sturtevant. *Pictorial History—Thirteenth Regiment Vermont Volunteers, War of 1861-1865.* No publisher cited, 1910, p. 291 and 317.
Second Lieutenant Joseph S. Milne, 1st Rhode Island Light Artillery
John B. Linn, diary, op. cit., p. 9.
Private Rufus S. Myers, 111th New York Infantry
Cornelia Hancock. H.S. Jaquette, editor. *South After Gettysburg....* Philadelphia, PA: University of Pennsylvania Press, 1937, p. 23.
Private William O. Doubleday, 14th Vermont Infantry
Horatio G. Jones, *To the Christian Soldiers and Sailors of the Union,* op. cit., p. 169.
Private Charles M. Lowe, 19th Maine Infantry
Horatio G. Jones, *To the Christian Soldiers and Sailors of the Union,* op. cit., p. 174.
Color Corporal Enoch K. Miller, 108th New York Infantry
Blake McKelvey (editor). *Rochester in the Civil War,* Rochester, NY: Rochester Historical Society, XXII, 1944, p. 171.
Captain James J. Griffiths, 72nd Pennsylvania Infantry
Robert Hubbard, M.D., unpublished letters, copies in the collection of the author.
Official Record of the War of the Rebellion, op. cit., vol. 27, part I, p. 700 and 707.
J. Howard Wert, "In The Hospitals of Gettysburg," op. cit., # 9.
Private Lewis Dellair, 125th New York Infantry
Charles W. Belknap, unpublished diary in the files of the Gettysburg National Military Park library.
Unknown Union Soldier
Mary C. Fisher, "A Week On Gettysburg Field," *Grand Army Scout and Soldiers' Mail,* vol. II, #12, 1883.

Gregory A. Coco, born in 1946, grew up in Mansura, Avoyelles Parish, Louisiana. He graduated from the University of Southwestern Louisiana in 1972 with a B.A. degree in history. From 1967 to 1969, Coco served in the U.S. Army, including a tour in Vietnam, where as an infantryman he was wounded twice. Since his return to civilian life, Coco has worked as a Louisiana state trooper, and as a park ranger, historian, maintenance worker, and licensed battlefield guide at the Gettysburg National Military Park.

Other books by the author:
Through Blood and Fire: The Civil War Letters of Charles J. Mills (1981); *On The Bloodstained Field* (1987); *A Vast Sea of Misery: A History and Guide to the Union and Confederate Field Hospitals at Gettysburg* (1988); *On The Bloodstained Field II* (1989); *Recollections of a Texas Colonel at Gettysburg* (1990); and *Wasted Valor: The Confederate Dead at Gettysburg* (1990).

Robert B. Moore has coupled thirteen years as a professional publicist with a love for history. A 44-year old native of Altoona, Pennsylvania, he has served as director of public relations for the NFL's Kansas City Chiefs since 1989, but has been associated with Gettysburg National Military Park in a myriad of positions since the mid-1970s. He acted as the Park's media information specialist from 1978-79, and directed its independent fund-raising efforts from 1985-89.

THOMAS PUBLICATIONS publishes books about the American Colonial era, the Revolutionary War, the Civil War, and other important topics. For a complete list of titles, please write to:

THOMAS PUBLICATIONS
P. O. Box 3031
Gettysburg, PA 17325

A Final Message To The Reader

I am a collector of the diaries, letters, and photographs of Civil War soldiers, which I use as research material for my books. If you or any acquaintance have such items for sale or loan, please write me at Bendersville, PA 17306-0400. Thank you.

Gregory A. Coco